Stanley Kubrick's *A Clockwork Orange*

Stanley Kubrick's *A Clockwork Orange* brings together new and critically informed essays about one of the most powerful, important, and controversial films ever made. Following an introduction that provides an overview of the film and its production history, a suite of essays examine the literary origins of the work, the nature of cinematic violence, questions of gender and the film's treatment of sexuality, and the difficulties of adapting an invented language ("nadsat") for the screen. This volume also includes two contemporary and conflicting reviews by Roger Hughes and Pauline Kael, a detailed glossary of "nadsat," and stills from the film.

Stuart Y. McDougal is DeWitt Wallace Professor of English at Macalaster College in Minneapolis. Former president of the American Comparative Literature Association, he is the author of *Made into Movies: From Literature to Film* and co-editor of *Play it Again Sam: Retakes on Remakes*, among other writings on film and literature.

THE CAMBRIDGE UNIVERSITY PRESS FILM HANDBOOKS SERIES

General Editor: Andrew Horton, *University of Oklahoma*

Each CAMBRIDGE FILM HANDBOOK is intended to focus on a single film from a variety of theoretical, critical, and contextual perspectives. This "prism" approach is designed to give students and general readers valuable background and insight into the cinematic, artistic, cultural, and sociopolitical importance of individual films by including essays by leading film scholars and critics. Furthermore, these handbooks by their very nature are meant to help the reader better grasp the nature of the critical and theoretical discourse on cinema as an art form, as a visual medium, and as a cultural product. Filmographies and selected bibliographies are added to help the reader go further on his or her own exploration of the film under consideration.

VOLUMES IN THE SERIES

Buster Keaton's "Sherlock Jr." ed. by Andrew Horton, Loyola University, New Orleans

Spike Lee's "Do the Right Thing," ed. by Mark Reid, University of Florida

Ozu's "Tokyo Story," ed. by David Desser, University of Illinois, Urbana–Champaign

"The Godfather Trilogy," ed. by Nick Browne, University of California, Los Angeles

Hitchcock's "Rear Window," ed. by John Belton

Godard's "Pierrot le Fou," ed. by David Wills, Louisiana State University

Buñuel's "The Discreet Charm of the Bourgeoisie," ed. by Marcha Kinder, University of Southern California

Bergman's "Persona," ed. by Lloyd Michaels, Allegheny College

"Bonnie and Clyde," ed. by Lester Friedman, Syracuse University

Stanley Kubrick's
A Clockwork Orange

Edited by

STUART Y. McDOUGAL

Macalester College

CAMBRIDGE
UNIVERSITY PRESS

CAMBRIDGE UNIVERSITY PRESS
Cambridge, New York, Melbourne, Madrid, Cape Town, Singapore,
São Paulo, Delhi, Dubai, Tokyo, Mexico City

Cambridge University Press
32 Avenue of the Americas, New York, NY 10013-2473, USA

www.cambridge.org
Information on this title: www.cambridge.org/9780521574884

© Cambridge University Press 2003

First published 2003
Reprinted 2009

A catalog record for this publication is available from the British Library

ISBN 978-0-521-57376-4 Hardback
ISBN 978-0-521-57488-4 Paperback

For Nora

Contents

Acknowledgments

My thanks to Andy Horton for stimulating discussions of this series when it was first being conceived and then to his extreme patience as this volume came to fruition. Jeff Middents, my research assistant at the University of Michigan, deftly and cheerfully locating stills and early reviews and essays on the film. Nora Gunnerg provided invaluable editorial support throughout. Gitta Hammarberg was extremely helpful in unraveling some of the difficulties of "nadsat" and in providing transliterations of the Russian etymologies.

The commissioned essays were for the most part finished before Kubrick's death in 1999. I held up the completion of the volume until the appearance of *Eyes Wide Shut* and then a professional move further delayed the publication of these essays. My apologies to the contributors for what became a long wait for the appearance of their work. Thanks, too, to Beatrice Rehl for her patience and helpful suggestions.

Contributors

Stanley Kubrick's *A Clockwork Orange*

STUART Y. McDOUGAL editor, is DeWitt Wallace Professor of English and Chair of the Department of English at Macalester College and the author of numerous works on film and modern literature, including *Made Into Movies: From Literature to Film* (Sixth printing, Harcourt Brace Jovanovich, Inc.); editor of *Dante Among the Moderns* (University of North Carolina Press); and co-editor, with Andrew Horton, of *Play It Again, Sam: Retakes on Remakes* (University of California Press). He is past president of the American Comparative Literature Association.

ROBERT KOLKER is now the Chair of the School of Communication and Culture at Georgia Institute of Technology after teaching cinema studies for over twenty years at the University of Maryland, College Park. His publications include *A Cinema of Loneliness: Penn, Stone, Kubrick, Scorsese, Spielberg, Altman* (now in its 3rd edition); *The Altering Eye: Contemporary International Cinema*; and *Bernardo Bertolucci*, all for Oxford University Press. Most recently he coauthored *Wim Wenders* with Peter Beicken, published by Cambridge University Press. He is also the author of *Film, Form and Culture: Text and CD-Rom*, published by McGraw-Hill. He is past president of the Society for Cinema Studies.

KRIN GABBARD is Professor of Comparative Literature at the State University of New York at Stony Brook. His most recent books are *Jammin' at the Margins: Jazz and the American Cinema* (University of Chicago Press), *Jazz Among the Discourses* (editor, Duke University Press), and *Representing Jazz* (editor, Duke University Press). He is currently writing a book on masculinity and the movies.

SHAILJA SHARMA is an assistant professor of English at DePaul University, Chicago, where she teaches modern British literature and postcolonial studies. She is working on a manuscript titled "Culture and Citizenship."

MARGARET DeROSIA graduated from the University of Michigan with highest honors in comparative literature. She is a Ph.D. student in the History of Consciousness Department at the University of California, Santa Cruz. Her dissertation, entitled "Detecting Desire: Women and Film Noir," examines women's role in shaping film noir on screen and in audiences.

JANET STAIGER is William P. Hobby Centennial Professor in Communication at the University of Texas – Austin and past president of the Society for Cinema Studies. Her recent work has focused on cultural and gender studies: *Interpreting Films: Studies in the Historical Reception of American Cinema* (Princeton University Press), *Bad Women: Regulating Sexuality in Early American Cinema* (University of Minnesota Press), and, most recently, *Perverse Spectators: The Practices of Film Reception* (New York University Press) and *Blockbuster TV: Must-See Sitcoms in the Network Era* (New York University Press).

PETER J. RABINOWITZ author of *Before Reading: Narrative Conventions and the Politics of Interpretation* and coeditor, with James Phelan, of *Understanding Narrative*, divides his time between music and narrative theory. His published articles cover a wide range of subjects, from Dostoyevsky to Mrs. E.D.E.N. Southworth, from detective fiction to the ideology of musical structure, and from Mahler to Scott Joplin. A professor of comparative literature at Hamilton College, he is also an active music critic and a contributing editor of *Fanfare*.

STUART Y. McDOUGAL

"What's It Going to Be Then, Eh?"
Questioning Kubrick's *Clockwork*

On March 7, 1999, Stanley Kubrick died at his home outside of London after nearly completing the editing of his final film, *Eyes Wide Shut*.[1] He was seventy years old and had lived a rather reclusive existence in England since 1974. *Eyes Wide Shut*, starring Tom Cruise and Nicole Kidman, was his first film in over a decade. Following several years of planning, the actual filming had occupied Kubrick and his stars for more than 15 months. Much fanfare accompanied its release in the summer of 1999 (Cruise and Kidman were on the July 5th cover of *Time* magazine), but the critical response was decidedly mixed, with some critics viewing it as a "haunting, final masterpiece" and others as a disappointment. Although Kubrick had prepared a final cut of the film before his death, the studio redefined the meaning of "final cut" by adding digitalized figures optically to obscure the explicit sexual activity of one of the film's central scenes before releasing the film in America. Kubrick's brilliant career ended with controversy and debate – characteristics that had marked his output at least since the release of *Lolita* (1962). Why did Kubrick's films – so varied and diverse – engender such heated discussion? Few directors of his stature have produced films that have consistently provoked so much controversy.

Stanley Kubrick began as a staff photographer for *Look* magazine at the age of seventeen. In part because of an indifferent high school record, Kubrick chose not to attend college. But it was a high school English teacher – Aaron Traister, whom he immortalized in a *Look* magazine photo spread in April 1946 – who ignited his interest in literature and drama. An immersion in films at the Museum of Modern Art inspired Kubrick to shift his focus from still photography to moving pictures. After making several documentaries and a low-budget feature financed by his family, Kubrick began to achieve recognition with his second feature, *Killer's Kiss* (1955), and his third, *The Killing* (1956). With *Paths of Glory* (1957), starring Kirk Douglas, he entered the ranks of America's most promising young filmmakers. His association with Kirk Douglas on *Paths of Glory* was to prove fruitful, for two years later, Kirk Douglas, by then the star and executive producer of the epic film *Spartacus*, hired Kubrick to replace Stanley Mann as director. This paved the way for an extraordinary outburst of creative work beginning with *Lolita* (1962). Kubrick moved into high gear with *Dr. Strangelove* (1964), *2001* (1968), and *A Clockwork Orange* (1971), three films later listed by the American Film Institute as among the top one hundred American films of cinema's first century. Each of these films provoked heated debate and each was a box-office success.

At the time of Kubrick's death, the most controversial of these films – *A Clockwork Orange* (1971) – was still unavailable in England, having been withdrawn from distribution by Kubrick in 1974. The novel, by Anthony Burgess, on which it was based, remained in print and in wide circulation. For Anthony Burgess, it seems in retrospect, Kubrick's movie was only the beginning of his obsession with this project. Unlike many novelists, who cash their checks and cease to ponder the fate of their work once it reaches the screen, Burgess continued to discuss his novel endlessly in essays, interviews, and letters to editors before reworking the material for two distinctly different musical dramatizations. The first of these, published in 1987 as *A Clockwork Orange: A Play With Music*, concludes with a character dressed like Stanley Kubrick coming out onto the stage with a trumpet, playing "Singin' in the Rain" until he is "kicked off the stage." A few years later, Burgess brought out yet another musical version, *A Clockwork Orange 2004*, this one produced by the Royal Shakespeare Company in London at the Barbican Theatre and featuring the music of Bono and the Edge. It too received very mixed reviews. For over a quarter of a century, then, Anthony Burgess reworked *A Clockwork Orange*, an obsession matched by few creative artists in this century. During this same period, audiences were unable to view the film in the country where it had been made. Why?

In the opening fifteen minutes of *A Clockwork Orange*, Kubrick confronts the viewer with a series of violent and sexually explicit scenes. In this respect, the film resembles the novel. But in the novel this material is narrated in a language of Burgess's invention. This language proves baffling to most readers and shields them somewhat from the sex and violence. No such distance is available to the film viewer. Although the British Board of Film Censors (BBFC) had rejected an earlier version of the script written by Terry Southern and Michael Cooper, they approved Kubrick's film and gave it an X rating on the grounds that the controversial materials were justified by the story. The film had already received this rating by the Motion Picture Association of America (MPAA) prior to its New York premier on December 20, 1971. Controversy did not end with the rating, however. In both England and America, conservative forces protested the showing of the film. A number of newspapers in America refused to take advertising for the film, prompting Stanley Kubrick to write the *Detroit News* a letter protesting the action and stating that "for any newspaper to deliberately attempt to suppress another equally important communications medium seems especially ugly and short-sighted."[2] In Britain, the Festival of Light, a conservative group promoting film censorship, organized a campaign to prevent *A Clockwork Orange* from being shown. The BBFC was forced to defend its decision to allow the film to be screened. The tabloids responded with attacks on the movie. In spite of the fact that *A Clockwork Orange* was receiving awards at festivals in Europe and America (Best Foreign Film at the Venice Film Festival, Best Film and Best Director by the New York Film Critics, and nominations for Best Film, Direction, Writing, and Editing at the Academy Awards), its distribution remained limited in both countries. Throughout 1972, *A Clockwork Orange* was shown at only one theater in London. In the United States, the X rating restricted distribution as well. Kubrick regrouped and took stock of the situation like a general planning for a long campaign. In August 1972, he announced that he was withdrawing the film in America for 60 days in order to reedit the work before resubmitting it to the MPAA. In October, Kubrick declared that he had replaced thirty seconds of film with less explicit material from the same scenes. His efforts resulted in a new rating (R) from the MPAA for this version. Both the R and X rated versions of the film continued to circulate in America as the controversy died down. In Great Britain the debates over the effects of film violence on viewers continued to rage. A rash of youth crimes was blamed on the maleficent influence of *A Clockwork Orange*. Kubrick was outraged. With little fanfare, he arranged – as owner of the British distribution right – to have *A Clockwork Orange* withdrawn from distribution in England. Although it remained widely available in America – in theaters and on video, laserdisc, and DVD – the film was not shown in England after its initial release. It was not until a year after the death of Kubrick that *A Clockwork Orange* received a major 250-print rerelease in Great Britain.

What did the forces of censorship object to in Kubrick's film? Even thirty years after its initial release, *A Clockwork Orange* continues to shock viewers, especially in its opening sequences. The film begins with the striking image of Alex de Large (Malcolm McDowell) seated on a banquette in the Korova Milkbar surrounded by his three "droogs" and enjoying some "moloko" spiked with "vellocet or synthemesc or drencrom" (milk mixed with drugs). The camera pulls back to reveal the Milkbar in all its splendor [Fig. 1]. This is one of the few sets created for the film (the others were found through a detailed study of recent issues of British architectural magazines) and the sculptures of nude women forming tables and milk dispensers

1. The Korova Milkbar in all its splendor.

establish an extremely disturbing tone for the film. After a few drinks, Alex and his droogs are ready for a "bit of the ultraviolence." What occurs in rapid succession is the brutal beating of a homeless man, an attempted gang rape that Alex and his droogs interrupt, and the pitched battle with the rival gang that follows. The sounds of a police siren bring this to an end, and Alex and his droogs quickly leave the scene, steal a car, and rush out of town, forcing other cars off the road as they race through the night. An illuminated sign, "HOME," catches Alex's eye and they stop before a modern structure. Once inside, Alex and his droogs brutally beat the aging writer and rape his wife while he looks helplessly on. Then it's back to the Milkbar for a nightcap before calling it a night. After returning to the bleak apartment block where he shares a flat with his parents, Alex calms his nerves by masturbating to "a bit of the old Ludwig van," a tape of the Ninth Symphony played at top volume in his small bedroom.

The next morning Alex skips school and is visited by his "postcorrective advisor," P. R. Deltoid (Aubrey Morris), who makes unsuccessful homosexual advances while Alex is getting dressed. Later, after a sexual interlude with two "little sisters" he meets at a music store, Alex joins his droogs at the Milkbar for another evening of fun. But the fun turns sour for Alex, as his authority is challenged by the gang, and he viciously attacks the three of them. Having reasserted his authority, Alex leads his droogs to another milkbar to prepare for what will be their last "bit of the ultraviolence" as a group.

At Georgie's suggestion, they drop in on "a very rich ptitsa" who lives alone at a "Health Farm" with her cats. Alex enters through a window and finds the middle-aged woman dressed in a leotard standing defiantly before him in a large room with sexually explicit paintings on the walls and a large sculpture of a phallus on the table. A battle ensues and Alex knocks her unconscious. (She dies later in the hospital.) The sounds of a police siren alert him to danger. As he leaves the house, he is confronted by his rebellious droogs. Dim smashes a bottle of milk on Alex's nose, and Alex falls to the ground screaming, "I'm blind, you bastards! I'm blind!!!" His companions flee and Alex is captured by the police.

I have described the first act of Kubrick's film (Chapters 1–7 in the novel) in some detail because the depiction of sex and violence here is responsible for most of the controversy surrounding the film. Critics have noted that Kubrick has changed the victims of Alex's crimes from Burgess's depictions, so that the crimes are somewhat less offensive to the viewer. Thus, while the violence directed against the homeless beggar in the film remains horrifying, it is less so than the encounter with the "doddery starry schoolmaster type veck" of Burgess's novel, a character who is encountered carrying "books under his arm" and "coming round the corner from the Public Biblio." Similarly, the intended victim of Billyboy and his droogs – "a weepy young devotchka. . . not more than ten" – has been transformed into a young woman in her late teens or early twenties. The two teenagers who willingly frolic with Alex after meeting him at the record store are – in the novel – younger girls whom he intoxicates and drugs before raping. And finally, the cat lady of the novel is an elderly woman "very gray in the voloss," living alone in a decaying house with her pets. In each instance, Kubrick has muted the horror by changing the nature of Alex's victims. More significant, however, are the ways Kubrick manages to distance the viewer from these horrendous crimes by choreographing many of these acts using music and/or slow motion photography. The effect of these techniques is to make the violence less real and easier for the viewer to follow on the screen.

The second and third acts of the film deal respectively with Alex's incarceration, treatment, release, suicide attempt, and "cure." There is relatively little sex and violence in these parts of the film and it occurs either in Alex's fantasies or in the movies he is forced to watch as part of his treatment. For many viewers, the incarceration and treatment of Alex by the state constitute the most dangerous violence in the film. In Kubrick's film, the Ludovico treatment becomes a metafictional moment that forces us to reflect on our own activity as film viewers. (This is not true of the novel, of course.) Alex too must become a film viewer, as part of his treatment, without the aestheticizing effects that Kubrick provides for his viewers in the first part of the film. In the fascistic world Alex has entered, he is forced to watch films as a way of programming him to find sex and violence nauseating in the extreme. The Ludovico treatment deprives him of any choice. This treatment, however, is presented in a cerebral manner, unlike the sex and violence that confront the viewer in the opening of the film.[3]

Anthony Burgess's novel reads like the report of a time-traveler who has landed on once-familiar terrain to find everything irrevocably changed. So must Anthony Burgess have felt when he moved back to London in 1960, after living abroad for a number of years in Singapore. With the Teddyboys in decline, Mods and Rockers were beginning to battle over turf and colonizers and subalterns alike were pouring into what had once been the capital of the empire, producing signs of the strains of immigration. Burgess had been diagnosed (incorrectly) by doctors as terminally ill and so – faced with what he thought was his imminent death and confronted by social decay and cataclysmic change – he wrote up a storm. By the time of his death thirty-five years later, he had authored over fifty books, including several studies of language. *A Clockwork Orange* (1962) is set in the Britain of the near-future and the work reflects the troubled state of England to which Burgess had returned.

The novel appeared to considerable critical acclaim, and the work's cinematic potential was readily apparent to many. Terry Southern, one of the screenwriters on *Dr. Strangelove*, personally optioned *A Clockwork Orange* for around $1,000 for a six-month period. He showed the novel to Stanley Kubrick who, according to Southern, was initially put off by the strange language. Southern renewed his option for another six months, wrote a screenplay with photographer Michael Cooper, and shopped it around. But he encountered problems with the British film censor, who returned the screenplay unread, with the comment that "there is no point reading this script, because it involves youthful defiance of authority, and we're not doing that."[4] When his option lapsed a second time, Southern didn't have the money to renew, so his lawyer, Si Litvinoff, picked it up and commissioned a new screenplay by Anthony Burgess. Litvinoff attempted to interest the Rolling Stones in the project, with the idea of Mick Jagger playing Alex and the Stones playing his sidekicks, the droogs. But the Stones were too busy to make a film and the project died, although Litvinoff and his partner, Max Raab, retained the rights to the novel.

At the time, however, Kubrick himself was occupied with other projects. After *Paths of Glory*, he turned to a book as controversial as *A Clockwork Orange*, Vladimir Nabokov's *Lolita*. This was followed by *Dr. Strangelove* and then *2001*. Each of Kubrick's subsequent films would be based on a work of literature and each of these works would present an entirely different challenge to the filmmaker. As Kubrick noted to Michel Ciment, "There is no deliberate pattern to the stories that I have chosen to make into films. About the only factor at work each time is that I try not to repeat myself."[5] With the enormous success of *2001*, Kubrick hoped to finance a film based on the life of Napoleon. He was obsessed with the project and extensively researched all aspects of Napoleon's military and political career, as well as his personal life. Kubrick discussed the project at length with Jack Nicholson, who began to share his enthusiasm and for whom the part of Napoleon would have been his first starring role. But in 1970 Sergei Bondarchuk's epic film *Waterloo* appeared, with Rod Steiger as Napoleon. Timing is everything, and with one film on Napoleon in the theaters already, financiers were reluctant to back another. Kubrick was forced to put his own ambitious project aside. He remembered the book Terry Southern had recommended to him earlier. He read it in one sitting and quickly decided that *A Clockwork Orange* would be his next film. According to Vincent LoBrutto, Litvinoff and Raab were happy to sell him the rights for around $200,000, which represented a nice profit for them, but no profit whatsoever for the author, Anthony Burgess.[6] Warner Brothers optioned the novel and Kubrick personally began to write the script. But the novel Warner Brothers optioned was the American edition of *A Clockwork Orange*, an edition that lacked the final chapter of the British edition.

Burgess had structured the novel into three sections of seven chapters each. In discussing the novel later, Burgess commented on the numerical symmetry and the significance of the number twenty-one as (among other things) the age at which one officially becomes an adult in the West. In one of the essays in this collection, Peter Rabinowitz considers the novel's "sonata" form with Chapter 21 as a sort of coda. Apart from questions of symmetry, however, the novel is very different when it ends with Chapter 20, as it did in all American editions prior to 1987. According to Burgess, his American publisher suggested deleting the final chapter and – eager to have the novel published in America – Burgess agreed. The final chapter takes Alex into adulthood and reformation. When asked about his choice of the American edition of the novel, Kubrick replied: "There are two different versions of the novel. One has an extra chapter. I had not read this version until I had virtually finished the screenplay. This extra chapter depicts the rehabilitation of Alex. But it is, as far as I am concerned, unconvincing and inconsistent with the style and intent of the book. . . . I certainly never gave any serious consideration to using it."[7]

Burgess's greatest achievement in *A Clockwork Orange* lies not in the story, however, but in the manner of telling it. For his novel, Burgess created a new language – which he calls "nadsat" from the Russian suffix for "teen" – comprised of a mixture of slang, baby talk, Romany, and Russian derivatives to express a reality that is at once near and distant.[8] (Not even Burgess could have predicted the fall of the Berlin Wall and the decline and dissolution of *that* empire. His use of Russian reflected his deep pessimism about the future of Great Britain.) Readers then – as now – recognize the society all too well while at the same time acknowledge its strangeness. This language was shaped by his great admiration for the work of James Joyce, as reflected in his two critical studies, *ReJoyce* (1965), an examination of Joyce's fiction, and *Joysprick: An Introduction to the Language of James Joyce* (1973), as well as in his edition of *A Shorter Finnegans Wake* (1967). In the midst of composing these homages to Joyce, Burgess decided to challenge Joyce's example by fabricating an English of his own. His creation of a credible language in *A Clockwork Orange* is, indeed, one of his greatest accomplishments as a novelist. And that accomplishment posed an extraordinary challenge for Stanley Kubrick.

When Alex is undergoing his Ludovico treatment, Dr. Brodsky, his psychologist, comments on his slang ("the dialect of the tribe") and then asks an associate, Dr. Branom, about its origins. Dr. Branom responds: "Odd bits of old rhyming slang. . . A bit of gipsy talk, too. But most of the roots are Slav. Propaganda. Subliminal penetration."[9]

Like James Joyce, Burgess wanted to create a new language so that it wouldn't appear dated. But the timeliness of the language is but one of its functions. The novel is related in the first person by Alex, a fifteen-year-old who lives in the indefinite future, with an immediacy and directness that draws the reader into the text. Alex speaks directly to us. His extraordinary command of language endears him to the reader as well.[10] In addition, the repeated use of "my brother" when addressing the reader (a variant of Baudelaire's famous line "Hypocrite lecteur – mon semblable – mon frère" ["Hypocritical reader – my likeness – my brother"]) and the many references to himself as "your humble narrator" together help establish an intimate relationship between Alex and the reader. We experience everything with Alex, and he shapes our perceptions. But Alex's language, like any foreign language, must be learned. Burgess clearly anticipated his reader's difficulties with the language. In the course of the novel, Burgess (through Alex) teaches the reader nadsat in a variety of ways, principally through context (e.g., "making up our rassoodocks [minds] what to do with the evening"), through the use of descriptive modifiers ("horn-rimmed otchkies" [eye glasses]), through the use of synonyms (e.g., "Our pockets were full of deng . . . But, as they say, money isn't everything"), and through repetition. When Alex kicks an enemy in the "gulliver," the meaning is unclear, but when Alex later receives a glass of beer with a "gulliver" on it, the reader understands that it means "head." Gradually the reader's difficulties with the language lessen. In the final chapter of the English edition (Chapter 21), we learn that nadsat has itself become dated, for the wife of one of Alex's former droogs is unable to understand him when he speaks and professes her amazement at its use. Nadsat does in fact intersect with a number of other dialects in the course of the novel, some of which the reader comprehends easily. Others, like the dialect spoken by the drugged customer in the Moloko Bar (Chapter 1), or the "old time real criminal's slang" of one of Alex's prison inmates (Part 2, Chapter 1), remain incomprehensible. To follow the novel, then, the reader must learn nadsat. Everything that happens is mediated through this language.

Nadsat functions in other ways as well. One of its principal uses is to distance the reader from the considerable violence of the novel, to act – in Burgess's words – as "a kind of mist half-hiding the mayhem."[11] The first third of the novel (Chapters 1–7) chronicle the "adventures of a young man who loves violence, rape, and Beethoven" (as the film poster proclaims) and it is no accident that this concentration of violence occurs when the reader is likely to have the most difficulty with the language. Consider Alex's narration of his outing with his droogs as they terrorize the writer, F. Alexander, and rape his unnamed wife:

> 'Drop that mounch. I gave no permission. Grab hold of this veck here so he can viddy all and not get away.' So they put down their fatty pishcha on the table among all the flying paper and they clopped over to the writer veck whose horn-rimmed otchkies were cracked but still hanging on, with old Dim still dancing round and making ornaments shake on the mantlepiece (I swept them all off then and they couldn't shake no more, little brothers) while he fillied with the author of *A Clockwork Orange*, making his litso all purple and dripping away like some very special sort of a juicy fruit. 'All right, Dim,' I said. 'Now for the other veshch, Bog help us all.' So he did the strong-man on the dvotchka, who was still creech creech creeching away in very horrorshow four-in-a-bar, locking her rookers from the back, while I ripped away at this and that and the other, the others going haw haw haw still, and real good horrorshow groodies they were that then exhibited their pink glazzies, O my brothers, while I untrussed and got ready for the plunge.
>
> (*Clockwork*, pp. 22–23)

Very few readers approaching the novel for the first time can make sense of that passage, expect perhaps for the final sentence. A second reading of the novel, however, is quite a different experience, for the language no longer shields one from the meaning and the horror of this scene is readily apparent.

Not only does Burgess create a special language for this novel, but one of the subjects of his novel is language. We see this through the intersection of nadsat and other dialects in the text. Many of the conversations are also in nadsat (nearly 90 percent of the nadsat terms are introduced in Part I), although this becomes less and less the case in Parts II and III. There Alex's interlocutors speak a variety of languages, but most of them are only slight variants on standard English. The focus on language is also manifested in the uses Burgess makes of readers and writers in his novel. The very first of his brutal encounters (Chapter 1) is with an elderly reader who is returning from the library ("Public Biblio") with a stack of books. Alex and his droogs tear up the books and beat the old man senseless. The old man reappears in Part III of the novel, when Alex goes to the library to seek information

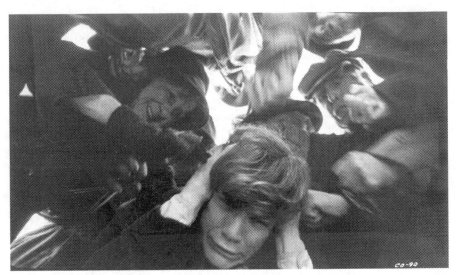

2. Alex (Malcolm McDowell) is attacked by the tramp and his friends.

on methods of suicide. He recognizes Alex and enlists the aid of his friends at the library to beat Alex brutally until the police intervene [Fig. 2]. The most vicious encounter of the first third of the novel and the one which proves to be a turning point in the final third is with "a writer not a reader" (p. 21) – F. Alexander, author of *A Clockwork Orange*, the title that Alex also gives to his own story.[12] Alex destroys Alexander's work and rapes his muse – a horrifying rape that results in her death. It is Alex's language – nadsat – that later identifies him to F. Alexander as the perpetrator of the earlier crimes (rather than his singing, as in the film).

In prison, Alex becomes a reader and later – after experiencing the events he chronicles in the novel – he becomes a writer as well. The transformation of Alex from brutal hooligan to writer is the greatest triumph of *A Clockwork Orange* and in one sense constitutes Alex's "final cure." That aspect of Alex's transformation is missing from Kubrick's film.

How does film – which mediates through the cinematic apparatus with language playing a supporting role – duplicate the linguistic effects of the novel? This was a concern Burgess had when he heard that Stanley Kubrick was planning to film *A Clockwork Orange*. In comparing his novel with *Lolita*, Burgess noted that. "I feared that the cutting to the narrative bone which harmed the filmed *Lolita* would turn the filmed *A Clockwork Orange* into a complimentary pornograph... The writer's aim in both books had been to put language, not sex or violence, into the foreground; a film, on the other hand, was not made out of words."[13] Kubrick succeeds in overcoming these challenges, and as a result Burgess became an enthusiastic and staunch defender of the film once it was released.

The film does utilize nadsat but in a very diluted fashion. Realizing that it would be impossible to teach the language to viewers in a short span of time, Stanley Kubrick retained enough of the language to create an unfamiliar effect but not so much as to confuse his viewers. He also simplifies the language and relies heavily on the Standard English of Alex's interlocutors. Compare the openings of the two works: The novel begins with a line that is repeated over and over: "What's it going to be then, eh?"[14] This question functions both as an invitation to the unknown and as a reassertion of the possibility of choice involving free will on the part of the readers – an issue that comes into question with the Ludovico treatment:

> 'What's it going to be then, eh?'
> There was me, that is Alex, and my three droogs, that is Pete, Georgie, and Dim, Dim being really dim, and we sat in the Korova Milkbar making up our rassoodocks what to do with the evening, a flip dark chill winter bastard though dry. The Korova Milkbar was a milkplus mesto, and you may, O my brothers, have forgotten what these mestos were like, things changing so skorry these days and everybody very quick to forget, newspapers not being read much neither. Well, what they sold there was milk plus something else. They had no license for selling liquor, but there was no law yet against prodding some of the new veshches which they used to put into the old moloko... which would give you a nice quiet horrorshow fifteen minutes admiring Bog And All His Holy Angels And Saints in your left shoe with lights bursting all over your mozg. Or you could peet milk with knives in it, as we used to say, and this would sharpen you up and make you ready for a bit of dirty twenty-to-one, and that was what we were peeting this evening I'm starting off the story with.
>
> (Burgess, p. 1)

Kubrick has two advantages that Burgess lacks in his novel: images and sound. Through the visuals, a convergence of signifiers conveys the meaning of the signified. When the film begins with the voice-over "There was me, that is Alex, and my three droogs, that is Pete, Georgie, and Dim and we sat in the Korova Milkbar," the camera first focuses on Alex in a close-up and then tracks back to reveal him surrounded by his three pals ("droogs") in what the viewer assumes is the Korova Milkbar. Through the visually established context, we understand the meaning of the dialogue. This is a mode of instruction unavailable to Burgess, but one that Kubrick uses adroitly. Moreover, Alex is established definitively as the narrator of the film. The viewer will experience the events of the film as Alex experiences them. But unlike the book, where everything is filtered through Alex's perspective – and nadsat is used consistently – the film maintains Alex's perspective by other than linguistic means. "Part of the artistic challenge," Kubrick explained to the *New York Times*, "is to present the violence as he [Alex] sees it, not with the disapproving eye of the moralist but subjectively as Alex experiences it."[15] Kubrick uses accelerated motion (the orgy with Alex and the two teenage girls), slow motion (some of the fighting sequences), and wide-angle lenses to achieve this effect. "I tried to find something like a cinematic equivalent of Burgess's literary style, and Alex's highly subjective view of things," Kubrick explained to Michel Ciment.[16] The electronic music score developed by Walter Carlos using the Moog synthesizer further contributed to the effect of defamiliarization sought by Kubrick. If, as Burgess noted, Kubrick failed in *Lolita* to find a cinematic equivalent for Nabokov's extraordinary prose, here he succeeds ably. Nearly thirty years after its release, *A Clockwork Orange* appears as fresh and challenging as when it first appeared.

The essays in this volume chart some of the major areas of contemporary inquiry into this masterpiece. Robert Kolker begins this section by considering one of the central issues in the long debates about *A Clockwork Orange*, the representation of violence in film. He places Kubrick's work within a history of film from the 1960s to the present. Although *A Clockwork Orange* has antecedents in the juvenile delinquent films of the 1950s, it "stands [this] genre on its head." Similarly, its use of violence marks it as very different from those violent films that directly preceded it such as *Bonnie and Clyde* (to which it was indebted) or *The Wild Bunch*. As Kolker demonstrates, *A Clockwork Orange* is equally different from the *Rambo* or *Die Hard* films that followed. But if *Bonnie and Clyde* succeeds in part "by reworking the current scene through the past," so Kubrick's film reworks the current scene through the future and it does this in a very self-reflective manner. What sharply differentiates *A Clockwork Orange* from other violent works for Kolker is its mise-en-scène, a mise-en-scène that is dominated by Alex and his remarkable voice. This mise-en-scène "foregrounds the artifice of the filmmaker's own work" and thus encourages "viewers to think about the ways the film construct[s] and then replace[s] the images of the world around us." This self-reflective film succeeds in part, for Kolker, precisely by forcing us to examine our "own notions of cinematic violence."

In "The Cultural Productions of *A Clockwork Orange*," Janet Staiger examines the varied effects of the film on contemporary viewers by placing "the U.S. public critical reception of *A Clockwork Orange* in parts of its cultural context." Her detailed and well-documented study "of the dynamics and tensions existing within the moment of the film's release" greatly clarifies the range and nature of the public's reaction to the film – and particularly to the issues of sexuality and violence. Staiger shows that the "effects of representation" became one principal line of argumentation as the film "entered the strands of discussion that had operated for centuries about obscenity and audience effect." The film was also attacked as "immoral," "misogynistic," and "misanthropic." The issues of Hollywood's negative influence and general immorality are still being debated in the Congress and Senate and have as much political force today as they did thirty years ago. But Staiger shows why they were so pertinent at that moment in history. It was the time of Vietnam and the protests of the 1960s; it was a time when foreign films had been appearing with increasing regularity on American screens; it was a time when Hollywood had adopted a new rating system for film. It was also a period when definitions of "obscenity" were being debated in the courts. Auteur film criticism and early feminist theory played roles in shaping the public debates over the film as well. Staiger deftly chronicles these developments and greatly clarifies the diverse contemporary reactions to this film.

Issues of sexuality and misogyny are considered in a very different light in Margaret DeRosia's "An Erotics of Violence: Masculinity and (Homo)Sexuality in Stanley Kubrick's *A Clockwork Orange*." Confronting a curious "silence over gender and sexuality," in

Kubrick's film, DeRosia asserts that any examination of the violence in the film must take issues of gender into account and in particular the film's construction of masculinity. DeRosia examines the instances of heterosexual sexuality and argues that they form "a prelude to or substitute for more meaningful (and homophobically inflected) sadomasochistic encounters between men." Indeed, the film contains "an unexamined but explicit link between free will or narrative agency and a highly virile and violent masculinity." In this context, De Rosia explores the implications of Alex as "at once both subject and object of the gaze, both active and passive psychic subject." Her astute analysis raises significant issues about spectatorship as well as about issues of gender and sexuality.

Krin Gabbard and Shailja Sharma consider Kubrick's film within the framework of high modernist art from Joyce to Beckett. They demonstrate that Joyce's *A Portrait of the Artist as a Young Man* is an important precursor to Kubrick's film, both in terms of thematic issues and the treatment of the protagonist as "artist-hero." Kubrick is shown to have more in common with high modernism in literature than with the European art films of the 1950s and 1960s. Gabbard and Sharma survey in detail Kubrick's innovative use of music in his films from his earliest works to *Eyes Wide Shut* and argue convincingly that he "reinstates the aesthetic ideals of Romanticism and Modernism in place of the more conventional 'invisible' score that marks mainstream film." With *2001*, Kubrick transformed the ways we think about cinematic soundtracks and he continues to refine this usage in *A Clockwork Orange*, thus providing another way of demonstrating his affinities with high modernism. The same could also be said of the highly mannered and self-conscious acting of *A Clockwork Orange* that has more in common with *Waiting for Godot* than the "more naturalistic, often self-effacing style of acting" that dominated Hollywood cinema. "The politics of *A Clockwork Orange*," Gabbard and Sharma conclude, "responds not to actual history but to the often solipsistic and contradictory but predominantly aesthetic projects of high modernist art."

Peter J. Rabinowitz considers both the novelistic and cinematic uses of music in "'A Bird of Like Rarest Spun Heavenmetal': Music in *A Clockwork Orange*." How, Rabinowitz asks, do you adapt an imaginary music that exists only on the printed page? This parallels the question of how you adapt a world described by a narrator who uses a fictional language (nadsat), and it leads Rabinowitz into yet another question: exactly what is involved when someone listens to music? By what codes does one comprehend what one hears? Rabinowitz presents a detailed and convincing explanation of this process before turning to an examination of the difficulties of adapting both fictive and real music to the screen. For Rabinowitz, the "imaginary music serves as a key element in Burgess's attempt to articulate his aesthetic position" and thus a great deal is at stake here. More is involved than just the search for an equivalent for imaginary music. Burgess was a composer with a voluminous knowledge of music and this knowledge informs and shapes *A Clockwork Orange* at every turn. Yet Kubrick – who prided himself on his knowledge of music and on the use of music in his films – "disregards musical distinctions that are central to Burgess's argument." Rabinowitz delineates Burgess's argument in great detail and then compares it with the "musical perspective" created by Kubrick "that is altogether different." The implications of this for our reading of the film are considerable.

Taken together, these essays – along with the reviews by the art critic and historian, Robert Hughes, and the film critic, Pauline Kael, included in this volume[17] – examine some of the major points of controversy and critical discussion raised by the film: the nature of cinematic violence, questions of gender and the treatment of sexuality, cinematic and literary antecedents of the film, the role of music in the novel and the film, issues of reception, and the difficulty of adapting an invented language and imaginary music. Clearly, the critical discussion of *A Clockwork Orange* shows no signs of abating.

NOTES

1 We may never know if Kubrick ever completed his work on *Eyes Wide Shut*. As Louis Menand noted ("Kubrick's Strange Love," *New York Review of Books*, August 12, 1999, p. 7): "Kubrick was exactly the kind of director who continues to drive everyone crazy with changes right up to opening night. It seems strange that he considered finished at the beginning of March a movie not scheduled for release until July." And Michael Herr (*Kubrick*, [New York: Grove Press, 2000]) states that Kubrick phoned him two days before he died and reported on the tinkering that remained to be done before the film was finished. See also Gabbard and Sharma in this volume.

2 Stanley Kubrick, quoted in James Howard, *Stanley Kubrick Companion* (London: B. T. Batsford, 1999, p. 129).

3 The use of Beethoven in *A Clockwork Orange* leads directly to Kubrick's last film, *Eyes Wide Shut*. Both films examine the nature of vision, of looking/seeing, of free will, and of directorial control (the two psychologists in *A Clockwork Orange* are surrogates for the director as are the characters Victor Ziegler, played by the distinguished director Sidney Pollock, and Red Cloak, played by Leon Vitali, in *Eyes Wide Shut*). Beethoven provides the crucial password that enables the hero of *Eyes Wide Shut* to enter the orgy that is one of the central scenes in the film. Kubrick draws ironically on the title of Beethoven's opera "Fidelio, or Married Love" ("Fidelio, oder Die Eheliche Liebe") for his password. See also my essay on "The Dream-Odyssey of Stanley Kubrick" in a forthcoming issue of *Cadernos de Traducão*.

4 Quoted by Terry Southern in Patrick McGilligan (ed.), *Backstory 3: Interviews with Screenwriters of the 60s* (Berkeley, CA: University of California Press, 1997, p. 394).

5 Stanley Kubrick, quoted in Michel Ciment, *Kubrick: The Definitive Edition* (New York: Faber & Faber, 2001, p. 153).

6 Vincent LoBrutto, *Stanley Kubrick: A Biography* (New York: Donald I. Fine, 1997, p. 339).

7 Stanley Kubrick, quoted in Ciment, *Kubrick* (p. 157).

8 See the Glossary for definitions and etymologies of nadsat.

9 Anthony Burgess, *A Clockwork Orange* (New York: W. W. Norton, 1986, p. 114).

10 In this sense he resembles another protagonist of dubious moral value, Shakespeare's Macbeth, who similarly enthralls the reader with his command of language.

11 Anthony Burgess, *You've Had Your Time: The Second Part of the Confessions* (New York: Grove Weidenfeld, 1991, p. 38).

12 The use of "orange" in the title of Alexander's work is another example of a slang (from *orang*, Malay for "man") that Alex later appropriates for himself ("like old Bog Himself . . . turning and turning and turning a vonny grahzny orange in his gigantic rookers" [p. 191]).

13 Anthony Burgess, *You've Had Your Time* (p. 244). Burgess's comment points to one of the central problems in Kubrick's *Lolita* – Kubrick's failure to capture Humbert Humbert's remarkable and distinctive mastery of English. We get little sense of Humbert as narrator of the film. In *A Clockwork Orange*, by contrast, Kubrick succeeds in creating a cinematic narrator who is part of the diegesis.

14 Although this line becomes associated with Alex, it is also repeatedly spoken by the prison chaplain (Part 2, Ch. 1).

15 Stanley Kubrick, quoted in Craig McGregor, "Nice Boy From the Bronx?" (*New York Times*, January 30, 1972, sect. 2, p. 13).

16 Stanley Kubrick, quoted in Ciment (p. 151).

17 These reviews by two distinguished critics represent the highly divergent reactions *A Clockwork Orange* elicited.

▌ *A CLOCKWORK ORANGE . . .* Ticking

In June 1995, Bob Dole – would-be president and a politician who has been insulated from the world for many years – attacked Oliver Stone's *Natural Born Killers* as a violent assault on Republican fantasies of home and family. The film, Dole said, is one of "the nightmares of depravity" created by Hollywood and popular culture that threaten "to undermine our character as a nation." In 1996, shortly before the political convention that nominated him, he praised Roland Emerich's *Independence Day* – a film that proposes, with all the manipulative advantages of the Hollywood style, now tricked up to digital perfection, pasteboard heroic figures fighting against evil alien invaders – as a film that upholds those values that Republicans hold dear.

When *A Clockwork Orange* appeared in 1971, it was attacked as an unmediated celebration of the violent young self, as a provocation to youthful viewers to imitate what they saw on the screen. There were – on the streets of England – acts of violence that seemed to be based on the film (just as there was at least one such act in the United States after the release of *Natural Born Killers*). A British judge – prophesying Bob Dole some twenty-five years earlier – said the film was "an evil in itself." Its creator, Stanley Kubrick, a man noted for his willful repression of a public persona, was moved to write a letter to the *New York Times* defending himself. Further, in concert with his distributor, Warner Brothers, he pulled *A Clockwork Orange* from British distribution. Despite some attempts to have it screened, and despite a Channel Four documentary that showed a lot of its footage (having won the right to do so in face of Warner Bros.'s lawsuit), it still remains unseen in England.

These are little vignettes from the ongoing narrative about how films influence the culture, a narrative whose subject is young people being made violent, forced into becoming desensitized to the world around them, and about the culture as a whole becoming demeaned by the films and television they watch. It's a particularly banal narrative (especially when it is inflected with right-wing discourse) because it ignores the complexities of cultural interactions and offers a one-way stream of influence from movie to antisocial acts. In the complexity of truth, popular culture exists in fairly thorough circulation of commodities and capital, in plain sight of all concerned. Cause and effect move in many directions. No one is innocent, and blame can be spread in many ways.

Because popular culture is, essentially, about commodities made for profit and purchased for pleasure, its products are not foisted on an unwilling and innocent audience by a conspiratorial culture industry. The culture industry is perhaps conniving and cynical, but it is certainly not a cabal out to ruin the nation's morals. This is not to say that a film is made without calculation. Quite the contrary. A film must be made by calculating in advance the kind of profit it will make. That calculation includes attempts to predict what an audience most wants to see. What's more, the audience is itself broken down – segmented – in order to predict what kinds of films some of its members want to see more than others.

A film, therefore, is one part of a complex swirl of influences and counterinfluences. A film's makers – studio executives, writers, agents, producers, actors, directors – work with a fantasy of audience desire and financial gain. They attempt to fashion a work that will meet with both and so call upon past films that did and look at the culture that surrounds them to find other clues to success. Most films are, therefore, amalgams – pastiches, if you will – of other films, of fantasies about why other films were successful, of guesswork at what will work again. Most films are created out of an economy of assent: everyone in the production process must agree (or be made to agree) on a work that everyone in the movie going public will, they hope, also agree on. Out of the cycle of assent will come, everyone hopes, a cycle of profit.

In the case of most films, this amalgamating, cyclical process feeds on a number of cultural constants and variables. The constants take the form of cinematic conventions: romance, fidelity, heroism, domesticity, individual initiative, and community spirit, colored in tones of sarcasm or sentimentality, but rarely irony. The variables are the contemporary twists put on the conventions, the individual narratives that retell the old stories, and refigure the old fantasies. For example, in the 1980s, in the culture at large, Ronald Reagan reworked a bizarre version of the myth of the frontier and the lone gunman. In response, movies invented Rambo, stalking the world, freeing souls from communist tyranny. But Rambo teetered on the edge of self-parody. Given the right ideological state of mind, fueled by a desire to fantasize victory in Vietnam and the belief that one well-muscled individual could destroy the country's enemies, the Rambo figure held out some hope. In other places, where Hollywood images were able to feed a vicious nationalism, it offered more than hope. Serbian weekend warriors in the former Yugoslavia dressed up like Rambo and went out to kill Muslims.

But in the United States, the figure was a bit too ludicrous, even if the convention of the lone hero was too precious to give up and even though Rambo himself entered the popular consciousness. The action hero got modified, by Arnold Schwarzenneger and, especially, by Bruce Willis, with touches of self-consciousness and even some irony. Violence became a game. Fed by images from video and computer games (beloved by the 15- to 25-year-old audience that Hollywood has been most interested in for decades) and a strongly developed understanding of the conventions of popular culture, filmmakers and audiences began to respond to the hero who could take his role less than seriously and engage in violent acts unscathed, but who prevailed nonetheless. Bruce Willis's John McClane in the *Die Hard* series (the name echoes John Wayne and a character named Jim McClain, played by John Wayne in a 1950s anticommunist film, *Big Jim McClain* [1952]) is all mock-serious and full of self-consciousness. The character is ironically aware of his own antecedents. "Who are you?" asks Hans, the bank-robber-cum-terrorist, "Just another American who's seen too many movies? Do you think you are Rambo or John Wayne?"

The *Die Hard* films want us to respond, "Well, yes, but of course not," as we cheer John McClane in his violent and heroic exploits. This self-mockery has complex consequences. It makes us knowing participants in the narrative; it allows us to scoff at the hero, recognize his fictive presence and his heroic ancestry, acknowledge the impossibility of any such character existing anywhere but in a movie, and affirm our desire that such a character might indeed exist to look after and excite us.

This entire process can be tracked along broader cultural movements of the 1980s. From Reaganesque gullibility (based on the despair that grew out of the assassinations of the 1960s and the Vietnam War and Watergate in the 1970s) to the development of a more self-protective cynicism in the late 1980s, the figure of violent action measured our unwillingness to give up fantasies of the heroic at the same time that we were giving up fantasies of the heroic. We paid a great deal of money to see these films (except in the cases of *Hudson Hawk* and *Last Action Hero*, where the parody and self-consciousness began to mock the audience), and so the Hollywood economy of assent was more than satisfied. We got to laugh at our own fantasies, and the filmmakers congratulated themselves on their good guesswork.

The action hero subgenre is dear to all concerned: it is at once too exaggerated and silly to be taken seriously; too attractive to ticket buyers not to be duplicated and reduplicated year after year; anonymous (who knows who directed *Rambo* or the *Die Hard* films?); and, most importantly, because of its parodic nature, unthreatening. These films provide us with satisfying images of violence that speak to us on many levels, but they are peculiarly quiet at the same time. They satisfy without intruding, without asking serious questions. That's why *Independence Day* was such a success. In spite of the growing self-parody within the action genre, there is still a need for the glow of the self-satisfaction of victory. There is also a need for a new enemy, now that "the Communist Menace" is no longer menacing. In the 1950s science fiction film, creatures from outer space were easy substitutes for invading Reds. Now, aliens are simply the form of an unnamable dread, which, when taken care of by a selfless and courageous African American Air Force pilot in a film whose rhythms and sounds move us through the inconsistencies of its narrative, allows us all to feel ennobled, though none of us has done a thing in the face of a film that manipulates us into assent.

What we are describing here is a spectrum of narrative construction and audience response, from the seamless ascendancy of the victorious subject in *Independence Day* through the self-conscious semiparodies of *Die Hard*. The more transparent the film, the fewer demands it makes on its viewers, and the more it affirms dominant cultural values, the more useful it appears. The more it points up cultural deficits and, most importantly, the more it jolts the viewer through stylistic peculiarities and narrative indirection, the more negative response it will get. This is the crucial point. Individuals – especially those with political power – rarely get upset over violent films. They get upset over films that ask questions about their violence and why we respond so eagerly to it.

This brings us back to *A Clockwork Orange* and its distant relative, *Natural Born Killers*. Both films are marked by a set of stylistic and personal imprints that take them beyond parody to political or philosophical statement. They are somewhat ambiguous in both their representation of violence and the response they ask us to take. They are films that address the politics and culture of violence through styles that are unusual and against the norms of Hollywood cinematic construction and that become problematic and even threatening. They tend to deflect concentration from the body of the hero and his marvelous exploits to the body politic itself, and they question why we need violent exploits at all.

A Clockwork Orange stands near the beginning of the current cycle of violent action films, following upon Arthur Penn's *Bonnie and Clyde* (1967, and another antecedent of *Natural Born Killers*) and Sam Peckinpah's *The Wild Bunch* (1969). But its antecedents could not be more different than the film of heroic exploit from which most current action films derive. Its antecedents (which it shares with *Natural Born Killers*) lie in the juvenile delinquent films of the 1950s, films like *The Wild One, Blackboard Jungle*, and *Rebel Without a Cause*. These films were born of a culture of confusion, a postwar uncertainty about the dissolving of communities, the growth of the corporate state, and fears of otherness and difference. They came, as well, from a growing respect of, and increasing fear about, the peculiarities of individuality development (exemplified by the Kinsey Reports on sexuality), a romance with Freudian theories of the family, an uneasy understanding of the "Oedipus complex," and a deep concern over who was responsible for the culture's social structure. The postwar period was confused by the anticommunist discourse that insisted any social commitment was tantamount to treason, and yet it was pulled by an ameliorating instinct, a desire for things to be better, easier. Tensions among rising financial resources coveted by middle-class consumers to enable them to buy property and goods, a fear of outside intervention by Russians and "communists," the dissolution of the central city and the extended family, a reexamination of gender roles, and utter confusion over who was in control of what led to a large cultural sense of displacement.

Part of that displacement, in the Freudian sense of moving a set of problems from their real site onto a surrogate site, occurred with teenagers, who, in popular culture, were made into representations of rebellion and violence. True to the period and the conventions of film, teenagers were more often than not shown as misunderstood, as victims of a society that could not cope with their energy or detect the troubled sensitivities that provoked their antisocial behavior. Movie teenagers, or juvenile delinquents (a term invented by postwar film, journalism, and congressional investigation committees), did damage, but it was proportional to the amount of misunderstanding and dysfunction in the culture around them. Jim Stark's cry, "You're tearing me apart," in *Rebel Without a Cause*, marked the dissociation of the sensitive young man both from the gangs and his henpecked father, and placed him within the realm of lonely young men who could not make their way in the postwar world.

Not all 1950s JDs were halfway to redemption, of course. The high schoolers in *Blackboard Jungle* are a fairly unrepentant bunch, and Lee Marvin's motorcycle gang in *The Wild One* seems to enjoy raising hell for the fun of it. But the Marlon Brando character in that film, the same one who, in response to the question, "What are you rebelling against?" answers "Whad'ya got?" is shown in tears when his frustrations and the misunderstanding of the people around him break through his defenses.

By the late 1950s, and into the 1960s, the juvenile delinquent began to disappear from the popular imagination and its representations. Adolescent crime, itself, did not disappear. In the darkness of the cities, the disaffection of the young, especially of marginalized Hispanic and African American youths, grew through the 1960s and continued to blossom, expanding to include suburban, middle-class white kids. As economic, racial, and cultural obstacles continued to rise above expectation and desire, and as city and suburb became spread further apart, juvenile violence grew.

But, from the perspective of popular culture, beginning in the 1960s, there was less interest in juvenile gangs and more interest in other representations of the ways adolescents behaved. The short-lived beatnik movement provided a bohemian and aesthetic expression of rebellion and disaffection during the 1950s. The Beats were a New York and San Francisco phenomenon and largely literary. They were associated with jazz and poetry, not the stuff of popular culture. Film and television only knew how to mock them (you can see the standard representation of the beatnik in the Vivian Darkbloom character in Kubrick's *Lolita*). The advent of rock-and-roll gave a larger geographical spread to adolescent expression and created a cohesion of adolescents that transcended space and class. That cohesion lasts until this day and has provided a rich source of imagery and narrative.[1]

The Beats, rock-and-roll, and politics merged in the 1960s into the hippie movement, which was more explicitly political than any youth movement that proceeded it. Because of its diversity and its politics, popular culture had a difficult time appropriating it. The difficulty was compounded by the expansion of the Vietnam War, the political demonstrations against it, and Richard Nixon's attempt to sublimate the rebellion against the war into a more abstract metaphor of "law and order," which, for him and his followers, identified hippies, drugs, sex, rock-and-roll, and political dissent with complex civil disobedience and a threat to the status quo.

Once more, the behavior of young people was turned to the advantage of political discourse, right-wing political discourse in this instance, that thrived by reducing cultural complexity to images that are comfortable and nonthreatening. This may seem contradictory when dealing with as explosive a subject as social disorder and masses of people rising up in the streets. But by abstracting it to a concept that many working and middle-class people could hardly deny, and by flattering those groups by recognizing them as a "silent majority" (for whom Nixon was supplying a voice), threatening behavior was turned on its head into its simple opposite. "Law and order" was an undeniable attraction to those whose children were being killed in Vietnam under the ideological imperative of defending one's country or were protesting the war in defiance of the ideological imperative of supporting one's country, right or wrong. Law and order is what would be restored under a Nixon presidency.

Juvenile delinquency had progressed in the popular and political imagination from a representation of rebellious, sometimes violent, teenagers to a threat to the very foundation of the culture. Adolescents and young adults were at the barricades and the government seemed helpless to stop them without resorting to a general call that implied major governmental controls.

There were a few films in the late 1960s that attempted to address the political uprisings of the moment. Most were unsuccessful. Even *Zabriskie Point*, made by the left-wing Italian director Michelangelo Antonioni – among the most important filmmakers of the decade – could not quite grasp the political complexity of the counterculture movement. However, Arthur Penn's *Bonnie and Clyde* was extremely successful by reworking the current scene through the past. Set in the South in the 1930s, it was able to create an allegory of contemporary youthful rebellion and position the viewer on the side of the rebels. It also happened to be the most graphically violent film ever made up to that time, and its attractive, vital characters are destroyed by that violence. *Bonnie and Clyde* reworked the juvenile delinquent film, caught some of the complexities of the youth culture of the 1960s, and created a dynamic spectacle that was simultaneously irresistible and appalling.

Bonnie and Clyde created a stir, but not the kind of social and political backlash of *Clockwork Orange* and *Natural Born Killers* – both of which it made possible. Because it was set in the past, because its radical and self-conscious style was used to forge a tight bond with its irresistible characters, and because that bond was brutally severed through the violent destruction of those characters, the film got sealed into the collective unconscious of its audience. The narrative and visual tensions between liberation and repression, expression and destruction were too strong to allow the film to be taken as a cultural assent to violent behavior. *Bonnie and Clyde* is simultaneously disturbing and soothing; it assures its viewers that they will lose the struggle, but the loss will be worth the energy expended to get there.

A Clockwork Orange does not coddle the viewer with such comforting ambiguities. Its celebration of unfettered energy seems quite straightforward. Its apparent thesis that unfettered free will, ex-pressed as violent disruption of other people's lives, is better than repression and a loss of freedom seems undeniable. What's more, its style and narrative structure keep the spectator in a position of awed conviction, distant and involved, amused and horrified, convinced and querulous, and at every moment involved.

By the time *A Clockwork Orange* appeared, Stanley Kubrick had al-ready proven his ability to make articulate spectacles and to discover in large, complex, tableau-like images a way to speak to and about the world at large. He had applied this talent to earlier issues of "law and order" – to gangsters (the adult versions of juvenile delinquents) in *Killer's Kiss* (1955) and *The Killing* (1956) and to the ideologies of class and combat in *Paths of Glory* (1957). He had confronted Ameri-can Cold War politics directly in *Dr. Strangelove* (1964), a rare film in which verbal spectacle was as strong as the visual. The language of *Dr. Strangelove* stands Cold War discourse on its head by exaggerating it beyond the limits of the serious. The result is a kind of verbal joust against the commonplace 1950s nonsense of communist subversion and the nonsense of missile gaps and atomic superiority.

The Cold War world comes to an apocalyptic end in the fiction of *Dr. Strangelove* through the inevitable self-destructiveness of its language. It would not overestimate the film to say that it influenced the slow demise of Cold War discourse in the culture at large. No one who responded positively to *Dr. Strangelove* and laughed at its manic parody of right-wing discourse could (in good faith) take seriously the real world's cautions about communist subversion and nuclear stockpiles.

Dr. Strangelove is the most straightforward of Kubrick's films be-cause its satiric trajectory is well marked, its targets unmistakable, and its desired effect on the viewer calculated and sure. *2001* (1968) and *A Clockwork Orange* are not that simple. They are denser, visually more complex, and considerably more ambiguous than their prede-cessors, especially on the subject of violence. Both films take violence not only as their thematic base, but as their political and cultural core as well. In these films, Kubrick sees violence as a kind of pri-mary, aggressive communication between individuals, cultures, and technologies; as a transitional point between historical moments; and as the major tool of politics. His idea is turned into a metaphor in the most audacious edit in film history: the cut between the ape's bone-weapon and the spaceship in *2001*.

In that cut, Kubrick suggests that all progress is based on, marked by, and articulated through violence, which he defines both as physical harm done upon one physical body by another, as well as the manifestation of power, cunning, manipulation, and blind obedience to a self-defeating cause. In *2001*, violence is inverted after the "Dawn of Man" sequence. The neurasthenic response of his space travelers to the spectacles of the universe bespeaks a repression of violent urges that reemerge only when the tools of technology assert themselves to protect their own interest. The revolt of the computer, HAL, and his murder of Poole and the hibernating astronauts represents a kind of transference of violence from the human body to its cyborg surrogates, an extension of the doomsday machine that destroys the world in *Dr. Strangelove*.

In *A Clockwork Orange*, doomsday has come and gone; the world remains physically intact, but the body politic has gone awry – though only slightly more awry than it is in "the real world." Student rebellion, the movement that had catalyzed the "law and order" rhetoric in the United States in the late 1960s (and the Mod and Rocker riots that had marked the most recent manifestation of class struggle in England, where Kubrick lived and worked), has here metamorphosed into rampant adolescent thuggery. The cultural landscape has itself degenerated into a kind of general, eroticized slum. The working-class housing projects (or "council houses" as they are called in England) are in a state of wreckage, their walls covered with vulgar graffiti. The local hangouts sell drugs – "moloko plus" – dispensed from the nipples of statues of naked women [Fig. 3].

The well-to-do live in spare, modern quarters outside of town, and there is a sense in the film's visual spaces of a limited, strongly class-determined, corrupt, and sterile world, sullen and withdrawn, fearful and drained of vitality. Except for three things: the language used by Alex and his associates, the language of the camera and lighting that create and control the physical spaces of the film (its mise-en-scène), and the physical violence Alex performs on everyone he can.

Kubrick stands the juvenile delinquent genre on its head. The misunderstood vulnerable young male in rebellion against a boring and

3. Dim (Warren Clark) helps himself to some of the "old moloko" at the Korova Milkbar.

repressive middle class has here become an exuberant, ironic, and self-aware young man at first in control and then controlled by a government that does the repressing and makes its people boring. Alex's energy comes from his physical presence and his ability to use it as intimidation and destruction. It comes from the way Kubrick sees – and allows us to see – Alex, especially in the first part of the film: in control of the frame, dominating space, he is the source of all activity. And the energy comes from the way Alex talks. His loquacious, rhythmic, image-filled language – created by Anthony Burgess, the author of the novel on which the film is based, and constructed out of a combination of English, Russian, and Cockney slang – drives and is driven by Alex. Alex's language, his insistent, seductive, cajoling, conspiratorial, jolly, threatening, self-pitying, and always ironic voice, becomes part of the film's mise-en-scène. And it is the mise-en-scène – of which Alex's voice is a part – that sharply differentiates *A Clockwork Orange* not only from its generic forebearers, but from most other films about violence ever made.

A Clockwork Orange is an antirealistic film. That is, it works against the usual codes of framing, cutting, narrative construction, character formation, viewer positioning, and thematic conventions that we take so much for granted when we watch a film. In ordinary films, the realistic style seems to erase those very structures that create it and the screen becomes a kind of transparent window onto an illusion of an ongoing world. Kubrick, along with a very few other filmmakers, undoes many of the premises of cinematic realism and forces us to take some things less for granted, to look at the film as a formal construction of meaning and ideas that may not be what it first appears, to confront some ambiguities. Through the film's hard, fluorescent lighting, the extravagant camera movement, which alternates with large, wide-angle tableaux, and its carefully figured, sometimes abstract and almost always metaphoric sets, *A Clockwork Orange* becomes a kinetic and meditative mechanism. It rushes us through its story and at the same time welcomes us to pause and think upon it.

Even the film's choice of music sets up an impossible dichotomy. Alex loves Beethoven, and he has violent fantasies as he listens to it. Classical music – not rock-and-roll – provides a background throughout the film. Purcell, Rossini, Elgar, as well as Beethoven, accompany Alex throughout his acts of "ultraviolence," except when he sings "Singin' in the Rain" as he maims the writer and forces him to watch the rape of his wife [Fig. 4]. The civility of the classical score, and the movie tune we all love, is used to surround the brutality of the modern world, much as the Nazis used classical music to mask their violence. It also allows us to reflect on the bizarre contradictions of Alex's character and echoes the symmetry of the narrative, which presents an artificial construct of rise, fall, and resurrection.

A Clockwork Orange lives up to its title in both form and content, working like a well-tuned mechanism. The first part of the narrative winds up Alex's violent excesses, climaxes in his capture and imprisonment, reaches a level state during his stay in jail, and begins unwinding through the Ludovico treatment – in which Alex is conditioned to become violently ill in the face of violence. The unwinding of the narrative reflects, almost sequence by sequence, the first part of the film. Only now Alex becomes the victim of his previous victims. A reversal seems to occur when, driven to attempt suicide by enemies of the state, Alex is rehabilitated by the Minister of the Interior, who has decided to use Alex for his own political ends.

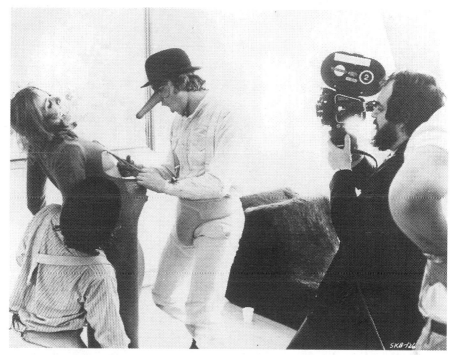

4. Kubrick films Alex (Malcolm McDowell) performing "Singin' in the Rain."

The result of this artificial, clockwork construction is a kind of tension that brings almost every statement and certainly the conclusion of the film into question. Its scenes of violence, its tracing of the cycle of Alex's ascent, fall, and rebirth, indeed everything, including its premise that free will is better than a controlled state of consciousness, is reflexive and full of doubt. Rather than "an evil in itself" as that British judge commented when *A Clockwork Orange* first appeared, the film is an ambiguity in itself and a provocation to the viewer to understand how "evil" may be understood or misunderstood.

This will be clearer if we focus on the main character. Alex is quite clear about his status as a fictional character. One reason for his unflagging irony is due not only to the fact that he knows how things will work out but also because he knows that he has been endowed by his creator with a sharp consciousness of his own mise-en-scène and his existence as a fiction. "There was me ... that is, Alex ...," he says in his first voice-over, as the camera tracks back from his glowering stare in the Korova Milkbar. It's as if he were looking at the footage, commenting, assuring, threatening. Early in the film, coming home after his night of brutality against the writer and his wife, he walks through the graffiti-fouled foyer of his council flat. The main theme of the film is playing on the sound track. Alex is whistling. He whistles the exact same tune. Alex exists on the image track; the music exists on the sound track. Both tracks are artifices, synthetic creations of light and sound, and here they merge, Alex aware of both at every turn.

His voice is present in every sequence of the film. He is the focus of our perception, and his words, climbing in ecstatic dominion, conniving to create mayhem, pleading for our pity, and, at the end, trumpeting his apparent rebirth and triumph, guide our responses. The film begins with a close-up of Alex's leering face, the camera tracking back to reveal him and his droogs in a tableau of sweet threat in the Korova Milkbar. His voice-over narration – omniscient, omnipresent – tells us who he is and what his plans are. He takes us into his confidence; he makes us confidants; he addresses us as "oh my brothers." His body is central to the frame: leering, fighting, beating people up, raping, masturbating, daydreaming, being tortured, drowning, falling out a window, lying in a hospital bed, making love in the snow – Alex's body is the organic mechanism in the film's clockworks.

The oxymoron is important: the body acts, reacts, and does damage to others, but the bodies in the film are mechanical, by definition unreal, because this is a film, not the world, and because everyone in it acts as if driven by some monomaniacal or inexplicable external force. Through the artifice of Kubrick's mise-en-scène, the symmetry of the narrative, and the peculiar interface created by Alex's voice-over, the unreality is heightened. The Korova Milkbar is an obvious set. The drive of the droogs through the night, playing "hogs of the road," is set obviously against a rear-screen projection. The fight with Billy Boy's gang is a staged, balletic performance [Fig. 5]. The appalling attack on the writer and his wife is again staged and exaggerated not to diminish its horror, but to offer perspective on it. The murder of the Cat Lady is intercut with images of her paintings mediated by the metaphors of the sculpted penis wielded by Alex and

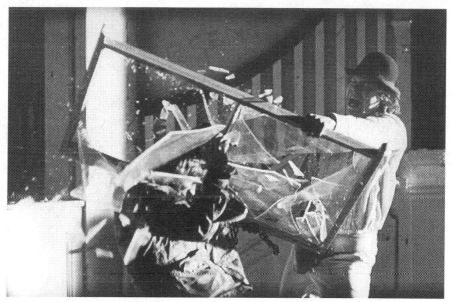

5. Dim smashes a window to the accompaniment of Rossini.

the bust of Beethoven she uses to defend herself. Indeed, perspective and mediation is what Kubrick is always offering: quite literally in his use of a wide-angle lens throughout the film, which causes the image at the sides of the frame to appear to veer off and makes close-ups of faces bulbous and distorted, and quite figuratively in his use of metaphor and irony.

This artificiality is doubly articulated. The film is set in a fantasy future and in turn sets itself up as a meditation on what that future might look and sound like. It requests that we, as viewers, take up its meditation and gaze at it with a certain distance, even as we are caught up in the kinetics of violence Kubrick creates. Within this artifice, Kubrick sets up an artificial moral dilemma. The mise-en-scène in which Alex is the main performer, owning the space within which he moves, moving us with his words and actions, ultimately traps him. He loses control of his space when he is jailed and undergoes the Ludovico treatment, which turns him into a cringing, puking wimp. During this sequence – the end of which has Alex performing his new self literally on a stage – the prison priest argues on Alex's behalf, presenting an apparent moral structure for *A Clockwork*

Orange. He suggest that free will and moral choice, even if used for evil, are better than a will controlled and molded to the needs of the state.

The choice seems irresistible, if complex. Of course free will is the most desirable component of human behavior. But do we need to choose between a selfish will to violence and a will controlled by political necessity? Are there other options? What is free will, after all? More and more, we are coming to understand that freedom, individuality, and subjectivity are not natural, but are instead historical and cultural constructs, the results of centuries of consensus and the discourse of power.

The film does not answer these questions overtly or covertly. It actually, by all the means of its artifice, tempts us to agree with Alex and the priest. Other possibilities – not alternatives, solutions, or even options – but other questions are obliquely posed first by the film's manipulation of cinematic and narrative space and second by opening up another space for contemplation. For one thing, the film quietly questions whether the obvious options are correct. Do we actually need to choose between Alex as brute and Alex as victim? Does Alex ever exercise free will? In the good tradition of the juvenile delinquent film, he seems very much a "product of his environment," one more stain of violent graffiti on the culture's wall, "a product of modern age," as the liberal intellectual, whose wife Alex has raped, suggests. This poor man is no more attractive than is Alex. As soon as he realizes that Alex was the transgressor, he forgets his liberal leanings and drives Alex to attempt suicide. No one in the film is attractive in the ordinary cinematic sense. They are stupid, venal, funny, helpless, or brutal. They all act out of need or corruption or a love of violence and power.

There are, finally, no choices available to anyone in the world of *A Clockwork Orange*. Everyone manipulates everyone else, Alex most of all. He is a product of the modern age, a victim of the state thrice over: once as a raging "free spirit," then as a cowering, brainwashed dupe of the state, and then – because it's politically convenient – a raging spirit, not "free," but placed at liberty to rape and pillage once again. Choices, the film finally suggests, lie somewhere else, perhaps in our own notions of cinematic violence and our belief that they reflect the external world.

Alex supplies a key to this reading. He and his creator know – seemingly better than we do – about the construction of reality, how we agree to the reality of what we see, and how the cinematic image first creates and then affirms our ideas of the world. "It's funny," he says in a voice-over during the Ludovico technique, as he shown images causing him to associate (like normal people) violence with revulsion. "It's funny how the colors of the world only seem really real when you viddy them on the screen."

Kubrick lets the secret out with this line. It is the code to this machine that seems to instruct its viewers to respond with terror and amusement to grotesquely violent events, presented in large, spectacular strokes, as if they were in some way mirrors of the world we live in. They are not, of course, mirrors. They are ideas, mediations, and representations of ways of being and thinking. They are also a lie. The world is a violent place and getting more so. Some governments are cynically manipulative and destructive of their people. But we do not live in a world where the choice is between Alex the killer and Alex the brainwashed wimp. The film only makes us think we do.

"I was cured, all right." These are Alex's final words to us. After he has been sent the other way through the Ludovico technique, so that he is now his old violent self – this time in service to the government. He says this over a bizarre image, a low-angle shot of himself making love to a woman in the snow, while people in top hats look on and applaud (some odd allusion to the Ascot sequence of *My Fair Lady*, perhaps). "I was cured, all right." He almost laughs and growls out the words, as if telling us he is back on the loose, ready for action. But not quite. Alex is a beast, but an owned beast, still a victim of the modern age, working for the state. Our beast.

A Clockwork Orange is, finally, a work of irony. It invites us to take multiple views of its subject, to take pleasure in the representation of a world which, if it actually existed, would cause us to flee in terror and therefore to admit to its artificiality.

Irony is not highly prized in commercial filmmaking. Because it asks viewers to hold a number of points of view simultaneously it is believed by most filmmakers to be too demanding. The responses requested by an ironic perspective are too uncertain, and irony disallows redemption. The British judge, who called *A Clockwork Orange* "an evil in itself," and Bob Dole, who called *Natural Born*

Killers a nightmare of depravity, wanted to escape the ironies and the self-reflexive stances these films take. They ignored how these films foreground the artifice of filmmaking and ask their viewers to think about the ways film construct and then replace the images of the world around us. But most of all, they did not find redemption in these films, and it made them nervous.

NOTES

1   Rock-and-roll was a part of the 1950s juvenile delinquent film. Bill Haley's "Rock around the Clock" was the title song for *Blackboard Jungle*.

JANET STAIGER

2 The Cultural Productions of *A Clockwork Orange*

This is Stanley Kubrick. He produced, wrote the screenplay for and directed *A Clockwork Orange*. I'm not sure that Kubrick sees himself as a practitioner of the Ludovico Technique, but I think he comes very close. Has it occurred to anyone that, after having our eyes metaphorically clamped open to witness the horrors that Kubrick parades across the screen, like Alex and his adored 9th, none of us will ever again be able to hear "Singin' in the Rain" without a vague feeling of nausea?[1]

– Susan Rice

What precisely might be the effects of watching *A Clockwork Orange* has preoccupied several decades of film scholars. Does the film romanticize and then excuse violence? Could it create a questioning of authorities? Is its effect more devastating, as Susan Rice suggests: the unsettling of a pure pleasure in watching Gene Kelly dance? And why did *A Clockwork Orange* become such a favorite among the cult audiences of the 1970s and later?

This essay will not answer any of these questions. What it will attempt is to place the U.S. public critical reception of *A Clockwork Orange* in parts of its cultural context with the hope that understanding some of the dynamics and tensions existing within the moment of the film's release will provide a description of some associations available to a film viewer of the era. These contextual associations would have a bearing on eventually answering questions about effect.

The critical reception of *A Clockwork Orange* has been studied with rather more detail than most other films. This is undoubtedly because of the public debates it generated within weeks of its U.S. release with an X rating and its actual censoring in Britain. A particularly good synopsis of the U.S. reaction occurs in Ernest Parmentier's summary of the criticism of *A Clockwork Orange*. Parmentier describes the initial laudatory praise of the director Stanley Kubrick and the film, followed by denunciations of both by Andrew Sarris, Stanley Kauffmann, Pauline Kael, Gary Arnold (of the *Washington Post*), and Roger Ebert. A series of letters in the *New York Times* also debated merits and deficits of *A Clockwork Orange*.[2] I will return to these public arguments below.

In Britain, where self-regulation and state regulation differ from that in the United States, government review of films occurred, with some films being considered by the regulators as unsuitable viewing fare and then prohibited from public screening. Guy Phelps explains that a conservative turn in the voting of 1970 encouraged a retightening of recent more liberal decisions. Thus, when *A Clockwork Orange* appeared, amid several other taboo-testing films such as Ken Russell's *The Devils* and Sam Peckinpah's *Straw Dogs*, the censoring board had a peculiar problem. Since the film itself criticized government attempts to control or condition youth behavior with the proposition that interference by authorities was more immoral than Alex's original behavior, it might look too self-serving of the Board to question the film. More importantly, however, demands by conservative commentators, requesting that the Board act against the increasing number and brutality of representations of violence on the screen, pushed the Board in the opposite direction toward acting against the film in some way.

Because the controversy seemed potentially damaging in the long-run, Kubrick convinced his British distributors to select a narrow release: the film was shown for over a year in only one West End London theater (although to large audiences).[3] When the distributors attempted a wider release at the end of that period, local activities of censoring had intensified. In February 1973, Hastings banned *A Clockwork Orange* on grounds that "it was 'violence for its own sake' and had 'no moral.'"[4] Other local authorities followed the Hastings' decision despite controversy in the public discussions.

The views that *A Clockwork Orange* presented "violence for its own sake" and "had no moral" were also major themes in the U.S. controversy and in that order. The first negative remarks were about the representations of violence. Sarris's review in *The Village Voice* in December 1971 describes *A Clockwork Orange* as a "painless, bloodless and ultimately pointless futuristic fantasy." Kauffmann, Kael, and Richard Schickel also attack the film for its representations of violence, warning that watching so much brutality could desensitize viewers to violence.[5] Thus, ad hoc theories of effects of representation became one line of argumentation, and *A Clockwork Orange* entered the strands of discussion that had operated for centuries about obscenity and audience effect.

The debates in the *New York Times* operated in philosophical and political discourses. What was the moral of this film? Was it moral? What were the politics of those praising or condemning the film? What are the responsibilities of a filmmaker? Kubrick and actor Malcolm McDowell participated in these discussions claiming that "liberals" did not like the film because it was forcing them to face reality.[6] Kubrick was particularly reacting to Fred M. Hechinger, who had charged that an "alert liberal...should recognize the voice of fascism" in the film.[7]

By the end of the first year of its release, a third line of attack opened on *A Clockwork Orange*. The film was accused of misogyny. Beverly Walker, writing in an early feminist film journal, charged the film adaptation with "an attitude that is ugly, lewd and brutal toward the female human being: all of the women are portrayed as caricatures; the violence committed upon them is treated comically; the most startling aspects of the decor relate to the female form."[8]

Within the context of the U.S. cultural scene of 1971–1972, that these three discursive themes – effects of the representation of violence, morality and politics, and gender relations – would come forth to be debated is easy to explain.[9] That they would be the staging grounds for a cult viewer's attraction to the film is also apparent. Precisely how these themes organized themselves in the debates is important to examine, however, for they take on a flavor peculiar to the circumstances of the era. The arguments in each of the three discourses were crossed by discourses related to (1) changing definitions of obscenity and pornography as a consequence of the sexual politics of the 1960s, (2) theories of audience effect, and (3) intertextual comparisons – interpreting the ideology of a film in relation to its source material.[10] In other words, the cultural productions of *A Clockwork Orange* were contextually derived but contradictory, and the consequence of the lack of an easy open and shut case about the meaning or effect or value of the film has been part of the explanation for the film's availability to so many people in so many ways.

EFFECTS OF THE REPRESENTATION OF VIOLENCE: TESTING DEFINITIONS OF OBSCENITY

At the time of the release of *A Clockwork Orange* in December 1971, a wave of films with scenes of violence were splashing across U.S. screens. In a preview article for the film, *Time* magazine had pointed to Roman Polanski's *Macbeth*, *Dirty Harry*, and the recent Bond film *Diamonds Are Forever* as part of a trend in which *A Clockwork Orange* was also participating.[11] Although some arguments could be made that these films were fictional responses to the nightly news images of Vietnam, two other, very salient, causal factors for the increasingly violent material were the previous twenty-year history of U.S. film exhibition and the changing laws of obscenity and pornography.

Since the end of World War II, foreign films were appearing with regularity on screens in larger U.S. cities; they were winning best film awards from U.S. and foreign critics and film festivals. Often, foreign films presented more sexually explicit images or dealt with seamier aspects of modern life, creating a stronger sense of verisimilitude (read as "realism"). Finally, broaching the boundaries of subject matter that had been considered off-limits by the Hollywood film industry was thus a competitive move by U.S. filmmakers against the foreign cinema. It was also a move of product differentiation against U.S. television, which had taken up the role of the family entertainer. During the twenty years up to 1971, Hollywood films had steadily penetrated earlier limits on sexual and violent materials. It had finally given up on the old production code's binary system of okay/not-okay, and in 1968 moved to a rating system organized by ages.[12] The G-GP-R-X system opened up possibilities of competition through subject matter in ways hitherto undreamed of. The possibility of such a system, however, required that previous definitions of obscenity and liability be changed before Hollywood could believe itself safe from criminal prosecution.

The representation of sexually explicit materials is not to be equated with the representation of violently explicit materials nor is either to be assumed obscene. However, the confusion of these notions was part of public protests of the 1960s. Those protests had to do with what counted as obscenity, and laws and discourses were in transition on this matter. In his excellent study of the history of pornography, Walter Kendrick traces the distinctions, and then confusions, between the terms "obscenity" and "pornography."[13] Kendrick argues that until the 1800s, Western tradition generally divided literature into serious literature and comedy. Serious literature had decorum, high status, and a public availability; comedy was abusive, low, and, if obscene, segregated into a nonpublic space. Obscenity could occur through use of both sexual and scatological materials.

It was not until the mid-1800s that "pornography" appeared, and at first it meant "a description of prostitutes or of prostitution," but also a "description of the life, manners, etc. of prostitutes and their patrons: hence, the expression or suggestion of obscene or unchaste subjects in literature or art."[14] Obviously, chaste versus lascivious representations of prostitutes could occur, and distinguishing between the two became important.

Now I would note here that although Kendrick suggests that obscenity had traditionally been located within the realm of comedy (and outside the field of serious literature), obviously images of eroticism have not always been deployed for a comedic effect; we would be naive to think that the nineteenth century invented representations designed for sexual arousal. What seems to be happening, I think, is that the term "obscenity" is being focused in its scope toward the sexual (and scatological), and its semantic field is redistributed in its scope to include not only sexually explicit materials for comedic effects but also erotic ones which did not, however, fit into traditional norms of serious literature. The project of categorization was confronted by ambiguous materials.

Moreover, soon theorists of law began to try to make distinctions between intent and effect when asked to rule on the categorization of instances of reputed obscenity or pornography. Here theories of audience effect entered. The distinctions made are, in legal discourse, "tests," and legal tests began to be made on presumptions that images could have audience effects. Kendrick notes that Lord Chief Justice Cockburn concluded an important mid-1800s British decision, *Regina v. Hicklin* (1868), on obscenity with the test being whether there existed in the materials "the tendency to corrupt the minds and morals of those into whose hands it might come."[15] If the conclusion of the "Hicklin Test" was positive, then one could infer that the author's intentions had been obscene and the author would be judged guilty.

Now two obvious observations are apparent: one is that the materials are being assumed to be naturally readable as obscene or not; the second is that intent is being determined from presumed effect. The various gaps in reasoning in these two propositions are immense.

Although both British and U.S. law generally operated under the Hicklin Test during the 1800s, by the later years of the century, U.S. courts were increasingly sympathetic to claims that if the questionable item were "art," then it was excluded from judgments of obscenity.[16] In other words, U.S. law began to rewrite the traditional binary categories of serious literature and comedy, with the opposition becoming serious literature/art versus nonserious (e.g., cheap) literature/not-art, and obscenity was only possible in the instance of the latter. In 1913, Judge Learned Hand undermined the "transparent-reading-of-effect-proves-intent" assumptions of the Hicklin Test by separating audiences: a possible effect on underage individuals should not necessitate the general prohibition of an item. It could be available privately, if not publicly, to mature readers. The effects of the troublesome representation were not universal or necessarily degenerate. In some sense, Judge Hand creates a "Selected-Effect Test."

Beyond the new, legal categorical separations of art versus not-art and universal versus select (and, hence, public versus private), U.S. law added a third new binary: the Part-Versus-Whole Test. The courts decided a 1922 case by the argument that although parts of a book might be lewd, the "whole" book was not; the "whole" book was art. If the whole book were art, then the power of art would override the effects of the segments of obscenity. Again, audience effects were significant in the test but refinements in assumptions of effects were occurring.[17]

These U.S. trends in regulating sexual materials explain why the U.S. ruled *Ulysses* (and *The Well of Loneliness*) could be published far earlier than Britain did. It is also the fact that, as a consequence of these tests, U.S. courts delegated pornography to the category of not-art. In 1957 the Roth Test became the new statement of the evolving semantics and theory of effect: "to the average person using community standards" would the dominant theme of the item appeal to prurient interests? In this test, the work is judged as a whole, and the United States as a whole is the community doing the judging. Moreover, obscenity is reduced to sexual content although not all sexual content is obscene (it is not obscene if it is in art). Obscenity is not protected by free speech, but obscenity is now "material which deals with sex in a manner appealing to prurient interests."[18] While the Roth Test opened up some types of material – the U.S. Supreme Court cleared physique magazines (which were often used as erotic material by gay men) of obscenity charges in the early 1960s[19] – the test also tacitly reduced obscenity to sexual content (although likely scatological material would also be considered). The 1973 refinement of the Roth Test by the Miller Test included not only the Whole-Item Test, but added the query of whether sexual conduct was represented in a "patently offensive" way.[20]

In this stream of shifting semantics about obscenity were the cultural, political, and sexual debates of the 1960s: the anti-Vietnam War crisis pitted free-love flower children against gun-toting war militants. "Make love not war" introduced a binary contrast that paralleled the question addressing why it was that sexuality was deemed by authority figures as offensive enough to be prohibited from view, whereas violence was not. Wasn't violence and its representations equally or probably more obscene? If sexual content might have harmful effects by appealing to susceptible minds, so might violent images.

Thus, at a time of increasing leniency toward (or means to justify) the representation of sexuality, political differences turned attention toward other subject matter that had only recently also been increasingly portrayed in public sites. Alongside the debates on what constituted obscene materials grew the arguments that representations of dominance by one person over another (rapes, objectification of individuals, and so forth) fit the category of "patently offensive" and had a potential to produce harmful effects (a continuation of the Hicklin Test).[21] Thus, antipornography feminists were not objecting to sexual content but content representing violence and arguing for its categorization as obscenity and for its removal from the public sphere.

A Clockwork Orange entered into the late 1960s debates over re-defining obscenity to include not only hard-core pornography but also violence. While ultimately legally protected as a work of art, *A Clockwork Orange* was not protected in the sphere of public discourse. Thus, the discussion about the representations of violence in the film echoes the centuries-long debates over sexual obscenity.[22] Moreover, the film's violence was not isolated as in the case of other violent films being released at about the same time: *A Clockwork Orange* had sexual content completely interwined within its violence.

One of the major themes of the attackers of the representations of violence in *A Clockwork Orange* was that it, indeed, was not art but exploitation. It failed Judge Hand's Whole-Item Test. "Exploitation" was a film-specific term for cheap, prurient, patently offensive, and – a sure sign it was not art – commercially driven. Examples of these criticisms include remarks such as in *Films in Review* that the film "sinks to the depths of buck-chasing (sex scribblings on walls; total nudity; sight-gags for perverts)."[23] Schickel agrees, defining the film as "commercial cynicism," and David Denby calls it a "grotesque extension of the youth movie" (also not art in 1971). Kael points out that in one scene the film opens on the rival gang's attempt to gang-rape a young girl so that, she underlines, more of the stripping can be shown: "it's the purest exploitation."[24]

In these attacks over to which category the film belongs – art or not-art – operate not only discourses concerned with the changing definitions of obscenity and theories of audience effect but also discourses of intertexual comparison. In the criticisms of its representations of violence (and in the ones on the film's morality and its gender politics), a major strategy of both attackers and defenders is to compare and contrast the source material with the film. Here the source material is Anthony Burgess's novel, *A Clockwork Orange*. With the development of auteurist criticism in the 1960s, the film *A Clockwork Orange* also becomes Stanley Kubrick's film. Thus, attributions of authorship and intent in these comparisons reduce to how

Kubrick changed (or did not change) Burgess's work. In the claim that the film's representations of violence classified it as exploitation not-art, attackers used the intertextual-comparison strategy. For example, Kauffmann notes that Kubrick changes the woman whom Alex assaults with one of her favorite art objects from "an old woman to a sexy broad [sic] and [kills] her with a giant ceramic phallus (thus changing sheer heartlessness into sex sensation)."[25] With the tacit proposition that the original novel is art, evidence of Kubrick's sexualization of the content proves that Kubrick's film is exploitation and not-art [Fig. 6].

Those criticizing the film for its representations of violence not only tried to define it as not-art but also argued that the representations had harmful effects and passed the Hicklin Test. Kael probably is relying on contemporary social science theses that proposed that individual experiences with violent images were not specifically harmful but repeated exposure to such images would eventually be bad

6. Auteur Kubrick and sexual violence.

when she rejected the idea that violent images were only reflecting reality; instead, she claimed they were "desensitizing us."[26] Vincent Canby somewhat responded to Kael by writing that although he was not disturbed by the violence, he could believe that this might not be the case for "immature audiences" (the Selected-Effect Test).[27]

Some people, of course, disagreed with those criticizing the film on the basis of its representations of violence. In these cases, the writers were attempting to establish *A Clockwork Orange* within the category of art and, consequently, not degenerate or obscene in its depictions of violence. If it was art, then the overall effect of the film was an art effect, which de facto would not harm its viewers.

The ways to defend the film as art were similar to the ways to attack it. Kubrick himself defended the film via the intertextual-comparison strategy; he claimed, "'It's all in the plot.'"[28] Others argued that the violence was justified realistically. Hollis Alpert points to the film's realistic connections among "the growth in youthful violence, the drug cultures, and the extraordinary increase in eroticism." Others took what Paul D. Zimmerman aptly describes as a "mythic realism" approach: the characters are caricatures, but of "some more basic essence."[29]

A third strategy to make the film art, beyond the intertextual-comparison approach and the realism argument, was the aesthetically motivated thesis. If a critic examined the images of violence in the film, the critic could discern formal and stylistic patterns, a sure sign of "art" and not exploitation. Canby writes, "the movie shows a lot of aimless violence – the exercise of aimless choice – but it is as formally structured as the music of Alex's 'lovely lovely Ludwig van,' which inspires in Alex sado-masochistic dreams of hangings, volcanic eruptions and other disasters." Cocks in *Time* claims the violence is "totally stylized, dreamlike, absurd." Alpert believes, "in lesser hands, this kind of thing could be disgusting or hateful, but curiously, as Kubrick handles it, it isn't. For one thing, the stylization throughout is constant." Mythic realism becomes universality: "Imagery, the kind that mythologizes and endures, is the nucleus of the film experience," claims *Playboy*'s reviewer.[30]

Thus, in the debates about the representations of violence in *A Clockwork Orange*, both sides of the discussion assumed several points: (1) Defining the film as art or not-art was important and

(2) determining the effects of the representations of violence had pertinence. Like the legal establishment of the era, these tests would determine how to categorize the film and evaluation would follow.

MORALITY AND POLITICS: READING THE IDEOLOGY OF A FILM

Although for years U.S. marxist critics had overtly been reading the ideology of texts and liberal reviewers had tacitly practiced this, numerous events of the 1960s increased tendencies to include these questions of content in evaluations of movie fare. These 1960s events included all those factors involved with the issues of representing sexuality and violence discussed above, but they also incorporated the implications of auteurist criticism and the move of film criticism into universities and colleges.

Within Western traditions of criticism, a debate has been waged between advocates who believe that human agency accounts for causality and those who stress the importance of social structures. This is often described as the humanist – structuralist debate. For most conservative and liberal commentators, the more prominent cause of events is human decision making; hence, Western literary tradition has so often stressed determining who created a work of art. This practice occurred in film criticism almost immediately at the start of the movies, but it certainly accelerated during the 1960s with the advent of auteurist criticism. Causes for auteurism include the influences of foreign art cinema and foreign film criticism, but defining films as art also permitted the wide introduction of film courses into colleges and universities. Moreover, studying contemporary culture as art (or at least as a reflection of culture) had relevance at a time when young radicals decried the staleness of the status quo institutions, which were often blamed for the public's lackadaisical attitude toward racism and the ever-deepening U.S. commitment in Vietnam.[31]

Trying to determine the authorship of a film, however, had consequences. Once agency can be pinpointed, so can blame. And, thus, locating in Kubrick (or Burgess) responsibility for representations raised philosophical and political issues of morality. Just what was the ideology the author(s) had presented? What were the implications of that ideology?

Both attackers and defenders of the film spent some space in the project of defining the meaning of the film. Burgess himself thought the meaning of the novel was about "the power of choice." Kael said the film's point was that "the punk was a free human being," while Schickel summarized the thesis as the "loss of the capacity to do evil is a minor tragedy, for it implies a loss also of the creative capacity to do good." Rice described it as "free choice must prevail/man's nature is perverse."[32]

No matter what the movie's thesis, one major strategy to absolve or blame Kubrick of responsibility for any potentially morally corrupt subject matter was the intertextual-comparison tactic. Critics who wanted to rescue the film argued that the novel was morally worse or that what Kubrick put in the film was already subtextually in the novel.[33] Critics who disliked the film, of course, found the differences from the novel proof of Kubrick's agency and his ideology. So both camps accepted Kubrick as author, used intertextual comparison to determine Kubrick's authorship, and then evaluated what they believed they had discovered.

The film's representation of Alex was one primary site around which this debate over ideology and morality focused. Both in the abstract and via comparison to the novel, reviewers thought Kubrick had created a central protagonist with whom the audience was to side. Alex "has more energy and style and dash – more humanity – than anyone else in the movie"; Alex might be compared with mass-killer Charles Manson, yet Alex is "surprising but undeniably engaging"; Alex is "more alive than anyone else in the movie, and younger and more attractive."[34] Those who appreciated this protagonist used Alex's representation to justify their respect for the film and to argue a positive moral message; those who did not appreciate this protagonist could also accuse Kubrick of using audience sympathy to make individuals morally complicit with an amoral message.

Indeed, the claims that the film was corrupt, unfair, and amoral were as many as the criticisms of its representations of violence and sexual attack. Kael was one of the first critics to pursue this line of denunciation. "The trick of making the attacked less human than their attackers, so you feel no sympathy for them, is, I think, symptomatic of a new attitude in movies. This attitude says there's no moral difference." The movie makes it too easy to enjoy or even identify with

Alex. He is given too many rationales for his behavior (bad parents, bad friends, bad social workers); he is cleaned up compared with the book's Alex; the victims are "cartoon nasties with upper-class accents a mile wide."[35]

Indeed, many of the criticisms in this range of discourse centered on not only whether Alex was made "too nice" but also whether Alex's victims were set up to be destroyed. Schickel's view is that "We are never for a moment allowed even a fleeting suggestion of sympathy for anyone else, never permitted to glimpse any other character of personal magnetism, wit, or sexual attractiveness comparable to Alex's. As a result, the film, though surprisingly faithful to the plot line of the novel, is entirely faithless to its meaning."[36]

It is in this group of responses that the accusation is made that the film is fascist. Hechinger's criticism derives from the series of propositions that if the theme is saying that humanity is inevitably corrupt, then this is authoritarian ideology. Jackson Burgess furthers that line, by arguing: "the laughter of *Clockwork Orange* is a mean and cynical snigger at the weakness of our own stomachs. . . . A strong stomach is the first requirement of a storm trooper."[37]

Not only was the protagonist too nice in contrast with the victims and the theme amoral or even fascist, but Kubrick's authorial voice was too distant and detached, making him doubly complicit with the theme. Kubrick is described as something of an amoral "god-figure" or a misanthrope. Kauffmann writes, "But the worst flaw in the film is its air of cool intelligence and ruthless moral inquiry because those elements are least fulfilled." Kael believes that the authorial voice is "a leering, portentous style," while Clayton Riley accuses Kubrick of "offer[ing] no cogent or meaningful commentary on [the violence]." Kubrick's authorship could have been redeemed, Denby thinks, had values been articulated by the end of the film, but "the mask of the ironist and savage parodist has fallen off, and behind it is revealed the fact of a thoroughgoing misanthrope." "How bored and destructive Kubrick seemed," concludes Seth Feldman.[38]

The conclusions about authorial view point were largely derived from two aspects of the film. One was the adaptation differences between the novel and the film, charged to Kubrick's decision making; the other was technical style. Part and parcel of auteurist criticism was a careful reading of stylistic choices, for, it was often claimed, the authorial voice of a director might be traced through style even if the director was compelled by studio or production circumstances to present a specific plot line. Here auteurist criticism provoked reviewers to read non-normative choices in mise-en-scène, camerawork, editing, and sound as from Kubrick's agency and also as meaningful in his expression of his position to the plot line he was, so to speak, given. Examples of such defenses have been provided above in relation to justifying the representations of violence as aesthetically motivated, including the classic auteurist praise of "consistency" of aesthetic design. The distance such an aesthetic choice produced could also be read as a protective device for the audience: the coolness provided for the audience a "resilence" needed to view the "multiple horrors."[39]

Critics of the film, however, connected Kubrick's stylistic choices with exploitation cinema (not-art). Jackson Burgess points out that "the stylization shifts your attention, in a sense, away from the simple physical reality of a rape or a murder and focuses it upon the quality of feeling: cold, mindless, brutality." Kauffmann writes that the camerawork was "banal and reminiscent" of many other recent films. Kael concludes, "Is there anything sadder – and ultimately more repellent – than a clean-minded pornographer? The numerous rapes and beatings have no ferocity and no sensuality; they're frigidly, pedantically calculated. . . . "[40] Kubrick's misanthropy, moreover, was also a misogyny.

GENDER RELATIONS: REVEALING SEXUAL POLITICS

The sexual revolution of the 1960s and the concurrent social and political upheaval had coalesced by the late 1960s. On the national scene feminists were criticizing canonical serious literature from perspectives of gender discrimination: Kate Millet's groundbreaking *Sexual Politics* appeared in 1969, and by the early 1970s, feminist film critics and academics were starting to read films ideologically for not only their moral or political politics but also their sexual representations. Joan Mellen's *Women and Their Sexuality in the New Film* was published in 1973, Marjorie Rosen's *Popcorn Venus: Women, Movies, and the American Dream* also in 1973, Molly Haskell's *From Reverence to Rape* in 1974, and Laura Mulvey's "Visual Pleasure and Narrative Cinema" in 1975.

In the second volume (1972) of an early feminist journal, Beverly Walker takes on *A Clockwork Orange*.[41] Her strategy is the same as the traditional auteur critic: she uses intertextual comparison with the novel and stylistic choices to conclude that Kubrick "has made an intellectual's pornographic film" (p. 4). Such a claim in 1972 needs to be recognized as a very powerful statement, given the debates about pornography and obscenity described above, and the militancy of feminists of the era. It should also, like the charge of "fascism," be understood as a rhetorical device agressively arguing for significant social and political change. Its communicative function is not only descriptive but also attention getting.

Walker's essay pinpoints numerous differences between the novel and the film, for the purpose, Walker argues, of making sex and genitilia more central to the film. The changes she describes include ones of mise-en-scène and plot. In the film, the outfits worn by Alex's droogs deemphasize the shoulders (as opposed to the costumes worn by the gang in the novel) and instead call attention to the male genitals, as the action shifts to include not only violence (as in the novel) but much more *sexual* violence. The Korova Bar is not described in the book; hence, the set design is Kubrick's fantasy. The characteristics of the women are changed from the novel. The novel's cat woman is older and lives in a house with antiques. When Kubrick introduces his catlady, she is shown in a grotesque yoga position, has a "phony, hard voice," and is surrounded by phallic and sexual décor – to invite, one might claim, sexual thoughts in the observers of the art objects. Such a decor and woman provide the classic excuse that the victim asked for the rape.

Not only is the cat woman redesigned, but Alex's mother is visualized. Walker believes that she is not dressed as befitting her age, although Alex's father seems traditionally clothed. The woman to be raped by the rival gang is clothed in the novel and also only a child (age ten) rather than being stripped naked and well endowed. Walker asks, "Why is it the women change radically in this Orwellian world, but not the men?" (p. 9).

The sexual design of the film does seem to have excited most of the reviewers (or their layout supervisors). The Korova Milkbar and Alex's close-up headshot are the favorite publicity stills to reproduce in articles about the film [Fig. 7 and Fig. 8]. Another favorite image is the scene of Alex's rectal examination by the prison guard, featured

7. The sexual mise-en-scène.

on the cover of *Films and Filming* for the issue that reviewed the film [42]
[Fig. 9]. That *Films and Filming* took such delight in the film seems to
confirm Walker's claim of a "homosexual motif" running through the
film since *Films and Filming* had a covert (or not so covert!) address to
gay men. Its review and selection of accompanying photos provides

8. The sexual mise-en-scène.

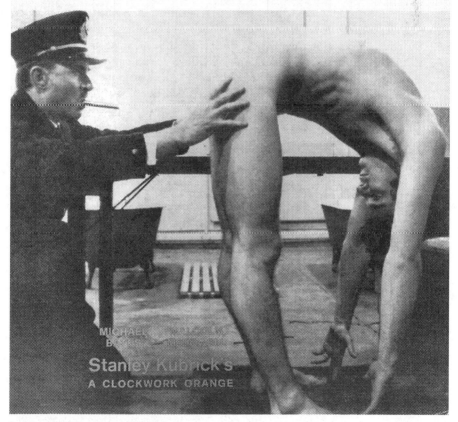

9. The examination of Alex.

ample evidence of another potential reading of the text, a point to which I will return below.

In conclusion, Walker suggests that the film is "woman-hating." As mentioned above, she believes it has "an attitude that is ugly, lewd and brutal toward the female human being: all of the women are portrayed as caricatures; the violence committed upon them is treated comically; the most startling aspects of the decor relate to the female form" (p. 4). The film is, again, exploitation: "all the naked ladies Kubrick has astutely used as commercial window dressing" (p. 4).

My review of the critical response to the film has focused to a large degree on the negative criticism; yet the film has become a cult favorite. Unfortunately, details of the fans' responses to the film could not be found. Still, speculation from the circumstances of the period and what became the focus of the critical response can give us some glimpse into what might have mattered to the early lovers of the movie.

Kubrick's authorial style was viewed by both supporters and critics as an aloof criticism of the social scene. Where one might put that authorial point of view in a range of political categories was debated, but without doubt, that point of view was considered iconoclastic. Such a nontraditional position has been appealing to most subcultural groups, of which cult viewers often align themselves. Kubrick's earlier work had already positioned him as out of the mainstream anyway: *Dr. Strangelove* was critical of every authority figure; *2001* immediately became a head movie. So when Kubrick's next film came out, antiauthoritarian adolescents were ready to take up the film anyway. The movie's flaunting of its representations of violence, sexuality, and sexual violence could be rationalized as realism or mythic realism and also enjoyed for their flaunting of recent obscenity and pornography taboos.

Additionally, in the late 1960s, film viewing audiences were well versed in several nontraditional strategies for watching films. One major viewing strategy had been the mainstream, "disposable" strategy in which seeing a film once is the norm. However, the concept and practice of repeat viewings of some movies had already become normative for two types of audiences: art-house devotees and underground/trash-cinema filmgoers. Both types of audiences rewatched films for several reasons: to find authorial signatures, to seek hidden messages, and to participate in a group audience experience.[43] While art-house and underground audiences often overlapped in terms of the actual people, differences in their makeup did exist and can be used to hypothesize their attraction to

A Clockwork Orange. Art-house audiences had been typed as "egg-heads" and were generally an intellectual crowd. Kubrick's work, with its complicated mise-en-scène and ambiguous message, fits well into the characteristics of an art-house film.

Underground cinema was more eclectic in terms of its audience, and because of the places and times where underground cinema was shown in the 1960s (run-down, large-city theaters; midnight screenings), underground cinema's audiences were very much an urban, mostly male, and gay or gay-friendly audience. Out of the rebel underground cinema of the 1960s, the mid-1970s cult classic *The Rocky Horror Picture Show* developed, with, at least initially, a strong gay participation. Now, I would not go so far as to suggest that more than a few audience aficionados of *A Clockwork Orange* read the film as camp, but that reading is, I believe, available from the sexual politics of the context and parts of evidence remaining (the *Films and Filming* "reading"). Moreover, the exaggeration of the mise-en-scène has echos to 1960s classic underground films such as *Flaming Creatures* (1963) and *Blonde Cobra* (1963). It is worth noting that Andy Warhol purchased the screenplay rights to Burgess's novel in the mid-1960s and produced his own adaptation of *A Clockwork Orange, Vinyl* (1965). Not surprisingly, *Vinyl* exceeds Kubrick's film in terms of the explicit sadomasochistic possibilities of the plot, but the general line of development is remarkably close to that of the novel, which suggests more credibility to Walker's thesis of the availability of a homosexual motif subtending the action.

Whatever the causes for the cult following of *A Clockwork Orange*, the density of reactions has perhaps also provided more avenues for speculating about violence, sexuality, morality, and gender politics. If Kubrick unwittingly participated with the authorities in his own version of the Ludovico technique, perhaps this was not the least valuable set of issues on which to inflict scholars and critics of cinema.

NOTES

1   Susan Rice, "Stanley Klockwork's 'Cubrick' Orange,'" *Media and Methods* 8, no. 7 (March 1972): 39–43.
2   Ernest Parmentier, "A Clockwork Orange," *Filmfacts* 14, no. 24(15 July 1971): 649–55. Also see Norman Kagan, *The Cinema of Stanley Kubrick* (New York,

NY: Grove Press, 1972), p. 182; Robert Philip Kolker, "Oranges, Dogs, and Ultraviolence," *Journal of Popular Film* 1, no. 3 (Summer 1972): 159–72; and Wallace Coyle, *Stanley Kubrick: A Guide to References and Resources*. Boston, MA: G. K. Hall & Co., 1980: 26–27.

3   Guy Phelps, *Film Censorship*. London: Victor Gollancz, 1975: 69–87. Also see Charles Barr, "*Straw Dogs, A Clockwork Orange* and the Critics," *Screen* 13, no. 2 (Summer 1972): 17–31.

4   Phelps, *Film Censorship*, p. 169.

5   Andrew Sarris, "Films in Focus," *Village Voice* 16, no. 52 (30 December 1971): 49; Stanley Kauffmann, "*A Clockwork Orange*," *The New Republic* (1 and 8 January 1972): 22 and 32; Pauline Kael, "Stanley Strangelove," *The New Yorker* 48 (1 January 1972): 50–53; Richard Schickel, "Future Shock and Family Affairs," *Life* 72, no. 4 (4 February 1972): 14.

6   Tom Burke, "Malcolm McDowell: The Liberals, They Hate 'Clockwork,'" *New York Times*, 30 January 1972: sect. 2, p. 13.

7   Stanley Kubrick, "Now Kubrick Fights Back," *New York Times*, 27 February 1972: sect. 2, p. 1.

8   Beverly Walker, "From Novel to Film: Kubrick's *A Clockwork Orange*," *Women and Film* 2 (1972): 4.

9   I am restricting this essay to the U.S. reception of the film. Phelps and Barr provide a valuable explanation of part of the British reception although more work could be done.

10 This observation has been stimulated by the recent reading of Walter Metz, *Webs of Significance: Intertextual and Cultural Historical Approaches to Cold War American Film Adaptations*. Unpublished Ph.D. dissertation, University of Texas at Austin, 1996.

11 Jay Cocks, "Season's Greetings: Bang! Kubrick: Degrees of Madness," *Time*, 20 December 1971: 80.

12 A good synopsis of this is in Garth Jowett, "'A Significant Medium for the Communication of Ideas': The *Miracle* Decision and the Decline of Motion Picture Censorship, 1952–1986," in *Movie Censorship and American Culture*, Francis G. Couvares, Ed. Washington, DC: Smithsonian Institution Press, 1996: 258–76.

13 Walter Kendrick, *The Secret Museum: Pornography in Modern Culture*. New York: Viking Press, 1987.

14 Kendrick, *Secret Museum*, p. 2.

15 Kendrick, *Secret Museum*, p. 122.

16 Kendrick, *Secret Museum*, pp. 174–187.

17 The events described here seem part of a larger trend in U.S. culture in dealing with regulating images. It parallels what I earlier observed happening with sexual images in the movies between 1895 and 1915. See Janet Staiger, *Bad Women: Regulating Sexuality in Early American Cinema* (Minneapolis, MN: University of Minnesota Press, 1995).

18 Kendrick, *The Secret Museum*, p. 201.

19 Martin Duberman, *Stonewall*. New York: Plume, 1993: 97. Also see Richard Ellis, "Disseminating Desire: Grove Press and The End[s] of Obscenity," in

Perspectives on Pornography: Sexuality in Film and Literature, Gary Day and Clive Bloom, Ed. New York: St. Martin's Press, 1988: 26–43.

20 Linda Williams, "Second Thoughts on *Hard Core*," in *Dirty Looks: Women, Pornography, Power*, Pamela Church Gibson and Roma Gibson, Ed. London: British Film Institute Publishing, 1993: 48.

21 These strands of argumentation reproduce themselves today with the new V-chip and television ratings systems.

22 These criticisms were not solely directed toward *A Clockwork Orange* but against the whole wave of violent movies appearing after 1967. See for example the reception of *Bonnie and Clyde*.

23 In researching the reception of *A Clockwork Orange*, I secured 57 reviews and articles published during the first two years of the film's U.S. release. In these notes, I shall cite only those items from which I quote or significantly paraphrase. H[arry] H[art], "A Clockwork Orange," *Films in Review* 23, no. 1 (January 1972): 51.

24 Richard Schickel, "Future Shock and Family Affairs," *Life* 72, no. 4 (4 February 1972): 14; David Denby, "Pop Nihilism at the Movies," *Atlantic* 229, no. 3 (March 1972): 102; Pauline Kael, "Stanley Strangelove," *The New Yorker* 48 (1 January 1972): 52.

25 Stanley Kauffmann, "A Clockwork Orange," *The New Republic* (1 and 8 January 1972): 22.

26 Pauline Kael, "Stanley Strangelove," The New Yorker 48 (1 January 1972): 53.

27 Vincent Canby, "'Orange'–'Disorienting But Human Comedy,'" *New York Times*, 9 January 1972: sect. 2, p. 7.

28 Stanley Kubrick quoted in Craig McGregor, "Nice Boy from the Bronx?" *New York Times*, 30 January 1972: sect. 2, p. 13.

29 Hollis Alpert, "Milk-Plus and Ultra-Violence," *Saturday Review* 54 (25 December 1971): 40; Paul D. Zimmerman, "Kubrick's Brilliant Vision," *Newsweek* 79, no. 1 (3 January 1972): 29; Robert Boyers, "Kubrick's *A Clockwork Orange*: Some Observations," *Film Heritage* 7, no. 4 (Summer 1972): 3.

30 Vincent Canby, "*A Clockwork Orange* Dazzles the Senses and Mind," *New York Times*, 20 December 1971, p. 44; Jay Cocks, "Season's Greetings: Bang! Kubrick: Degrees of Madness," *Time* (20 December 1971): 80; Hollis Alpert, "Milk-Plus and Ultra-Violence," *Saturday Review* 54 (25 December 1971): 40; "Kubrick's *A Clockwork Orange*," *Playboy* 19, no. 1 (January 1972):200.

31 Janet Staiger, "The Politics of Film Canons," *Cinema Journal* 24, no. 3 (Spring 1985): 4–23; David Bordwell, *Making Meaning: Inference and Rhetoric in the Interpretation of Cinema* (Cambridge, MA: Harvard University Press, 1989); Janet Staiger, "With the Compliments of the Auteur: Art Cinema and the Complexities of its Reading Strategies," in *Interpreting Films: Studies in the Historical Reception of American Cinema* (Princeton, NJ: Princeton University Press, 1992): 178–95 .

32 Anthony Burgess, "Clockwork Marmalade," *Listener* 87, no. 2238 (7 February 1972): 198; Pauline Kael, "Stanley Strangelove," *The New Yorker* 48 (1 January 1972): 50; Richard Schickel, "Future Shock and Family Affairs," *Life* 72 no. 4 (4 February 1972): 14; Susan Rice, "Stanley Klockwork's Cubrick Orange,"

Media and Methods 8, no. 7 (March 1972): 40. Ironically, some of the debate over the film's meaning reproduces issues in the humanist-structuralist debates which were, in fact, beginning to rage in academia at that time.

33   Arthur Gumenik, "*A Clockwork Orange*: Novel into Film," *Film Heritage* 7, no. 4 (Summer 1972): 7–18.

34   Craig Fisher, "Stanley Kubrick produces, directs 'Clockwork Orange,'" *Hollywood Reporter* (14 December 1971): 10; Jay Cocks, "Season's Greetings: Bang! Kubrick: Degrees of Madness," *Time* (20 December 1971): 80; Pauline Kael, "Stanley Strangelove," *The New Yorker* 48 (1 January 1972): 50.

35   Pauline Kael, "Stanley Strangelove," *The New Yorker* 48 (1 January 1972): 50–51.

36   Richard Schickel, "Future Shock and Family Affairs," *Life* 72, no. 4 (4 February 1972): 14.

37   Hechinger paraphrased in Stanley Kubrick, "Now Kubrick Fights Back," *New York Times*, 27 February 1972, sect. 2, p. 11; Jackson Burgess, "A Clockwork Orange," *Film Quarterly* 25, no. 3 (Spring 1972): 35–36.

38   Stanley Kauffmann, "A Clockwork Orange," *The New Republic* (1 and 8 Janaury 1972): 22; Pauline Kael, "Stanley Strangelove," *The New Yorker* 48 (1 January 1972): 52; Clayton Riley. ". . . Or 'A Dangerous, Criminally Irresponsible Horror Show'?" *New York Times*, 9 January 1972: sect. 2, p. 1; David Denby, "Pop Nihilism at the Movies," *Atlantic* 229, no. 3 (March 1972): 102; Seth Feldman, "A Clockwork Orange," *Take One* 3, no. 3 (April 1972): 21.

39   Robert Boyers, "Kubrick's *A Clockwork Orange*: Some Observations," *Film Heritage* 7, no. 4 (Summer 1972): 2. Also see Stephen Mamber, "A Clockwork Orange," *Cinema* [Los Angeles, CA] 7, no. 3 (Winter 1973): 48–57.

40   Jackson Burgess, "A Clockwork Orange," *Film Quarterly* 25, no. 3 (Spring 1972): 35; Stanley Kauffmann, "'A Clockwork Orange,'" *The New Republic* (1 and 8 Janaury 1972): 32; Pauline Kael, "Stanley Strangelove," *The New Yorker* 48 (1 January 1972): 50.

41   Beverly Walker, "From Novel to Film: Kubrick's *A Clockwork Orange*," *Women and Film* 2 (1972): 4–10.

42   *Films and Filming* 18, no. 5 (February 1972).

43   Janet Staiger, "With the Compliments of the Auteur," pp. 178–95; Janet Staiger, "Finding Community in the Early 1960s Underground Cinema," in *Swinging Single: Representing Sexuality in the 1960s*, ed. Hilary Radner and Moya Luckett (Minneapolis: University of Minnesota Press, 1999): 39–74.

BIBLIOGRAPHY

Alpert, Hollis. "Milk-Plus and Ultra-Violence." *Saturday Review* 54 (25 December 1971): 40–41, 60.

Barr, Charles. "*Straw Dogs, A Clockwork Orange* and the Critics." *Screen* 13, no. 2 (Summer 1972): 17–31.

Bordwell, David. *Making Meaning: Inference and Rhetoric in the Interpretation of Cinema*. Cambridge, MA: Harvard University Press, 1989.

Boyers, Robert. "Kubrick's *A Clockwork Orange*: Some Observations." *Film Heritage* 7, no. 4 (Summer 1972): 1–6.

Burgess, Anthony. "Clockwork Marmalade." *Listener* 87, no. 2238 (7 February 1972): 197–99.

Burgess, Jackson. "*A Clockwork Orange*." *Film Quarterly* 25, no. 3 (Spring 1972): 33–36.

Burke, Tom. "Malcolm McDowell: The Liberals, They Hate 'Clockwork.'" *New York Times*, 30 January 1972: sect. 2, p. 13.

Canby, Vincent. "*A Clockwork Orange* Dazzles the Senses and Mind." *New York Times*, 20 December 1971: p. 44.

Canby, Vincent. "'Orange'–'Disorienting But Human Comedy.'" *New York Times*, 9 January 1972: sect. 2, pp. 1 and 7.

Cocks, Jay. "Season's Greetings: Bang! Kubrick: Degrees of Madness." *Time*, 20 December 1971, pp. 80–85.

Coyle, Wallace. *Stanley Kubrick: A Guide to References and Resources*. Boston, MA: G. K. Hall & Co., 1980.

Denby, David. "Pop Nihilism at the Movies." *Atlantic* 229, no. 3 (March 1972): 100–104.

Duberman, Martin. *Stonewall*. New York: Plume, 1993.

Feldman, Seth. "*A Clockwork Orange*." *Take One* 3, no. 3 (April 1972): 20–21. *Films and Filming* 18, no. 5 (February 1972).

Fisher, Craig. "Stanley Kubrick produces, directs 'Clockwork Orange.'" *Hollywood Reporter*, 14 December 1971, pp. 3 and 10.

Gumenik, Arthur. "'A Clockwork Orange': Novel into Film." *Film Heritage* 7, no. 4 (Summer 1972): 7–18+.

H[art], H[arry]. "*A Clockwork Orange*." *Films in Review* 23, no. 1 (January 1972): 51.

Jowett, Garth. "'A Significant Medium for the Communication of Ideas': The *Miracle* Decision and the Decline of Motion Picture Censorship, 1952–1986," in *Movie Censorship and American Culture*, Francis G. Couvares, Ed., Washington, DC: Smithsonian Institution Press, 1955: pp. 258–76.

Kael, Pauline. "Stanley Strangelove." *The New Yorker* 48 (1 January 1972): 50–53.

Kagan, Norman. *The Cinema of Stanley Kubrick*. New York: Grove Press, 1972.

Kauffmann, Stanley. "*A Clockwork Orange*." *The New Republic* (1 and 8 January 1972): 22 and 32.

Kendrick, Walter. *The Secret Museum: Pornography in Modern Culture*. New York: Viking Press, 1987.

Kolker, Robert Philip. "Oranges, Dogs, and Ultraviolence." *Journal of Popular Film* 1, no. 3 (Summer 1972): 159–72.

"Kubrick's 'A Clockwork Orange.'" *Playboy* 19, no. 1 (January 1972): 200–205.

Kubrick, Stanley. "Now Kubrick Fights Back," *New York Times*, 27 February 1972: sect. 2, pp. 1 and 11.

Mamber, Stephen. "*A Clockwork Orange*." *Cinema* [Los Angeles, CA] 7, no. 3 (Winter 1973): 48–57.

McGregor, Craig. "Nice Boy from the Bronx?" *New York Times*, 30 January 1972: sect. 2, p. 13.

Metz, Walter. "Webs of Significance: Intertextual and Cultural Historical Approaches to Cold War American Film Adaptations." Unpublished Ph.D. dissertation, University of Texas at Austin, 1996.

Parmentier, Ernest. "*A Clockwork Orange.*" *Filmfacts* 14, no. 24 (15 July 1971): 649–55.

Phelps, Guy. *Film Censorship.* London: Victor Gollancz, 1975.

Rice, Susan. "Stanley Klockwork's 'Cubrick Orange.'" *Media and Methods* 8, no. 7 (March 1972): 39–43.

Riley, Clayton. ". . . Or 'A Dangerous, Criminally Irresponsible Horror Show'?" *New York Times,* 9 January 1972: sect. 2, pp. 1 and 13.

Sarris, Andrew. "Films in Focus." *Village Voice* 16, no. 52 (30 December 1971): 49–50.

Schickel, Richard. "Future Shock and Family Affairs." *Life* 72, no. 4 (4 February 1972): 14.

Staiger, Janet. *Bad Women: Regulating Sexuality in Early American Cinema.* Minneapolis, MN: University of Minnesota Press, 1995.

Staiger, Janet. "Finding Community in the Early 1960s Underground Cinema," in *Swinging Single: Representing Sexuality in the 1960s,* Hilary Radner and Moya Luckett, Eds. Minneapolis, MN: University of Minnesota Press, 1999: 38–74.

Staiger, Janet. "The Politics of Film Canons." *Cinema Journal* 24, no. 3 (Spring 1985): 4–23.

Staiger, Janet. "With the Compliments of the Auteur: Art Cinema and the Complexities of its Reading Strategies," in *Interpreting Films: Studies in the Historical Reception of American Cinema.* Princeton, NJ: Princeton University Press, 1992: 178–95.

Walker, Beverly. "From Novel to Film: Kubrick's *A Clockwork Orange.*" *Women and Film* 2 (1972): 4–10.

Williams, Linda. "Second Thoughts on *Hard Core.*" In *Dirty Looks: Women, Pornography, Power,* ed. Pamela Church Gibson and Roma Gibson. London: British Film Institute Publishing, 1993. pp. 46–61.

Zimmerman, Paul D. "Kubrick's Brilliant Vision." *Newsweek* 79, no. 1 (3 January 1972): 28–33.

3 An Erotics of Violence

Masculinity and (Homo)Sexuality in Stanley Kubrick's *A Clockwork Orange*

A symptomatic silence over gender and sexuality haunts analyses of Stanley Kubrick's 1971 film, *A Clockwork Orange*. Criticism of the film has tended to focus on three general areas – philosophical questions and concepts (i.e., free will and humanism), the film's representation of violence, and Kubrick as film auteur. These analyses frequently treat gender and sexuality superficially or ignore them entirely. In order to articulate its visual and thematic concerns, however, the film both supports and parodies the stability of (hetero)sexual difference. Because of this tension in representation, I want to consider the construction of gender and sexuality in the film and specifically explore the film's construction of masculinity.

Before beginning my analysis, I want to summarize briefly the three general areas of criticism mentioned above. First, the film's philosophical arguments on free will situate Alex's violent anarchism against the government and the Ludovico scientists' fascist attempts to control and contain him. Because the only sympathetic character is Alex, the film mobilizes support for anarchism over fascism by portraying the other characters as caricatures. Throughout the film, their hypocrisy undermines their credibility, leaving Alex in a position of relative moral and narrative authority.

This thematic and philosophical irony of the film has been a common area of exploration for several critics.[1] While *Clockwork* explores these issues, however, it also casts a critical gaze on the antihero, Alex. Thomas Allen Nelson, for example, does not characterize Alex's actions and subjectivity as ironic, but rather as straightforward and refreshingly normal. He writes:

> Alex works from the inside out – from fantasy to performance – as he transforms the lifeless settings and cultural mythology of an overly conditioned society into a new order of truth. . . . He does not separate mind from body, reflection from action, the unconscious from social reality; nor does he transfer his sexual or violent urges onto objects and become, like others, a voyeur of his own degradation.
>
> (p. 154)

Nelson's disturbing embrace of Alex's "new order of truth" is not necessarily reflected in the film, which treats ironically Alex's unrestrained libido, violence, imprisonment and conditioning, and certainly his "rebirth." Although *Clockwork* clearly mobilizes identification with Alex, it also demands a suspension of belief in the reliability of this "humble narrator."

A second and related type of criticism has also emphasized the film's irony and distantiation by focusing on its representation of violence.[2] Controversial since its inception, *Clockwork* has provoked a variety of responses ranging from vehement hatred to enthusiastic praise. While violence is a central element in the film, however, few besides Daniels have discussed the ways in which gender and sexuality influence Alex's "ultraviolence." Although Alex attacks both men and women, the kinds of violence he perpetuates are not analogous. Furthermore, any analysis of violence should take masculinity into account. Especially given the historical context of Vietnam, films with traumatized and violent male subjects should not be read as gender-neutral statements on violence; indeed, such films may target and traumatize male subjects with a greater intensity than female ones.

Perhaps as a backlash to the controversy over violence, another critical approach to *Clockwork* has focused on Kubrick's style as a film auteur. Auteur-theoretical analyses often overlap those mentioned earlier and are nuanced in stylistic and cinematographic detail. They draw upon Kubrick's reputation as a director who is highly involved in all stages of film production; indeed, each of Kubrick's films bears a characteristic look, regardless of genre. However, such analyses, in avoiding an uncritical celebration of Alex, do not address how Kubrick's images mobilize specific forms of spectatorial identification.

Given how *Clockwork* systematically establishes gender and sexuality as points of reference, such a critical silence on *why* it mobilizes gendered identities and identifications demands reconsideration. Few critics have outlined that gender is present in the film, and when they have gender has not been presented as a problem to be analyzed and explored.[3] If it is present, the film's supposedly more important arenas of philosophical/moral debate and directorial style override it. Gender, however, functions as more than a straightforward backdrop to *Clockwork*. From the opening tracking shot of Alex and his droogs [fellow gang members] at the Korova Milkbar, with "furniture" composed of naked female mannequins in sadomasochistic poses, to the rape sequences and attack on the Cat Lady, to Alex's post-Ludovico humiliation at the breasts of a naked woman onstage, to the film's final image of Alex and a woman frolicking in the mud before a crowd of enthusiastic Victorian spectators, the film's treatment of women is significant and problematic. Ignoring this aspect of the film's style or alluding to gender as unproblematic backdrop to ethics and aesthetics perpetuates the film's unexamined but explicit link between free will or narrative agency and a highly virile and violent masculinity. Masculinity thus becomes the default setting for an exploration of supposedly humanist concerns in a cinematic narrative.

Although critics have not explored the construction of masculinity in *Clockwork*, other Kubrick films – *Spartacus*, *Dr. Strangelove*, *2001*, and, most notably, *Full Metal Jacket* – have been subject to such analyses.[4] Such criticism has examined male homosocial conflicts and a sense of crisis in the consolidation of a male self. Many such studies employ arguments from Laura Mulvey's essay "Visual Pleasure in Narrative Cinema." In that essay, Mulvey argues that male anxieties sustained and resolved in narrative cinema deploy the subject of the gaze as male and the object of the gaze, the spectacle to be seen and investigated, as female (p. 19). Mulvey's critics have responded with questions such as: what happens, however, when the male subject becomes the object of an intra- or extradiegetic gaze? Or why does masculinity, if it is secure in its authority, often rely on excessive displays of virility and violence in order to sustain, paradoxically, its aspirations to the normal?[5] As Cohan and Hark ask in their response to Mulvey's essay, "[W]hat are we to make of a masculinity that can preserve its hegemony only by confessing its anxieties at every turn?" (p. 2).

Clockwork takes pains to put Alex, and by extension, masculinity, through an extensive series of trials and challenges, which may or may not be "cured" by the end. Simply celebrating Alex as antihero avoids looking at the film's anxieties surrounding the stability of masculinity, a stability that can only be sustained by reference to sexual difference. Sexual difference is repeatedly undermined, however, by eroticizing the homosocial field at the expense of the heterosocial (as hetero*sexual*).[6] Heterosexual encounters like the rapes, the record store *ménage à trois*, and the mud wrestling finale are portrayed as less erotically cathected than, for example, the fight between Alex and his droogs and Billy Boy's gang, or Alex's post-Ludovico beatings.

The film's representation of heterosexuality suggests that heterosexual rape, violence, and even consensual sex are really diversions or, more radically, a prelude to or substitute for more meaningful (and homophobically inflected) sadomasochistic encounters between men. My reading of this structure of desire draws on Eve Sedgwick's *Between Men: English Literature and Male Homosocial Desire*. In her reading of various canonical English literary texts, homosocial desire is triangulated through the trope of two men attracted to the same woman. The men's rivalry generates a strong undercurrent of eroticism that only can be deflected through reference to the woman.

Clockwork employs similar strategies, but often, and more radically, completely eliminates the intermediary woman. In the film, homosocial relations are initially meetings among equals and/or rivals. Precisely because of this starting point, however, the playing field must be rendered unequal through violence. Given the greater eroticism and vitality with which violent contact is represented, however, sexual desire between men is the taboo the film disavows and reiterates in complex and ambivalent ways. Thus, the film maintains an ambivalent relation to women, sustaining their presence as objects of desire while debasing and denying them all subjectivity. Rather than dismiss *Clockwork* for its misogyny, however, I want to examine how misogyny is an effect of anxieties about masculinity. Furthermore, because these anxieties often are represented in highly self-reflexive conditions, the film evidences anxieties over specifically *cinematic* narrative constructions of the male subject.

Clockwork explores the link between masculinity, subjectivity, and violence by symptomatically representing these realms in highly (homo)eroticized, self-reflexive ways. In my analysis, I look at these tensions both before and after Alex's arrest and imprisonment. In the first section, I examine the opening tracking shot and how homosocial violence is represented within or against heterosexual violence in three of the gang's attacks. In the second section I look at the Ludovico "treatment" and its relationship to self-reflexivity. I also discuss the second HOME sequence and the film's conclusion. In spite of the sharp narrative break that marks the film's second half, *Clockwork* undermines as much as affirms masculinity's narrative authority. Ultimately the film deconstructs the link between vision and narrative mastery by repeatedly positioning Alex among other men as the feminized spectacle. While many critics have celebrated Alex's subjectivity and authority, few have highlighted that his position, tenuous from beginning to end, is treated with more irony and ambivalence than unqualified support.

"READY FOR LOVE ?": MASCULINITY'S HORRORSHOW

The opening tracking shot of *A Clockwork Orange* has often been discussed as a symbol of Alex's narrative mastery. Through the use of the voice-over, a standard cinematic technique for suturing spectatorial identification, Alex captivates us [Fig. 10]. He appears to be the

10. Alex's penetrating gaze.

11. Alex among his drugged droogs.

only character in this extended shot with the ability to look, for the rest of the characters are dulled by their consumption of "moloko-plus," a drugged version of milk. Alex's adversarial and sardonic gaze directly meets the camera. As the camera tracks back, Alex is shown situated with his three other droogs in a dark room [Fig. 11]. They rest on white "furniture" – naked female mannequins in sadomasochistic poses with near-orgasmic expressions, their long hair bright blue and red. Other people sit or stand in the room, but their drug-induced stillness make the furniture-women, in their state of sexual abandon, look more alive than their "real" human counterparts. Alex's voice-over, however, separates him from the others and situates him as the primary, active subject of the narrative.

Several aspects of this shot complicate Alex's prototypically mas-culine authority. In spite of his direct gaze and voiceover, he is also the object of the camera's gaze. In Mulvey's formulation of the look in narrative cinema, the camera's gaze allies the diegetic male character's look with that of the (implicitly male) spectator (pp. 25–26). In this opening shot, however, the film introduces a split between the gaze of the camera and the gaze of its antihero, Alex. Although Alex returns the camera's gaze, this first shot introduces a tension between the two looks, a point of disjunction that the film will repeatedly disavow in an effort to sustain Alex's narrative authority.

Furthermore, the opening close-up of Alex shows one eye adorned with false eyelashes and the other without. Through this mark of the feminine *on* the male body – men generally do not wear false eyelashes unless they are drag queens – the film signals an ironic link between masquerade and masculinity. This emphasis on the eye is linked to the bloodied eyeball "cufflinks" on Alex and his droogs' sleeves and foregrounds the self-reflexive dimension of the film, but not in a gender-neutral way.

I raise this point not in order to refute readings of the self-reflexive dimension of the film, but rather to point out the complicated interplay between the film's treatment of gender and its emphasis on self-reflexivity. Alex does achieve narrative authority in this opening scene, but only against a series of visual contradictions. The "women" of the Korova Milkbar ostensibly contrast Alex's masculine vitality and narrative authority. Alex's feminized eye, however, metonymically links him to the female furniture. Furthermore, the white shirts and pants both he and his droogs wear as part of their costume parallel and blend in with the porcelain white female furniture-figures upon which they sit.[7] Alex's classically masculine posture and narrative authority can only be achieved by placing him in a room full of lifeless "women" and frozen, silent men. Although the voice-over suggests narrative authority, Alex remains the object of the camera's gaze throughout the shot, physically diminishing in size through the backward tracking motion until the camera literally disembodies him. Thus, these tensions represents Alex's implicit polymorphous perversity. The opening shot not only establishes dual anxieties over what constitutes the human and sexual difference, but connects more specific thematic and visual concerns such as the relationship between power and gender differences, sadomasochism (itself the ultimate link between violence, power, and eroticism), and cinematic self-reflexivity.

I have focused on the conflation and contradiction of themes in the opening shot because the film explores and develops these themes throughout the diegesis. This tension in the first shot between Alex as masterful masculine subject and feminized object of the gaze parallels the tension between the film's highly erotic homosocial realm and its distanced, comical, and/or incidental representation of heterosexuality. The simultaneous disavowal and privileging of a homoerotic, violent masculinity over against a superficial treatment of heterosexual sex/rape can be witnessed in three of the film's first sequences of attack – Billy Boy's near-gang rape of a young woman, Alex and his droogs' attack of Mr. Alexander and his wife, and Alex's attack and murder of the Cat Lady. In each sequence, a predominantly heterosexual encounter becomes incidental to a more serious and meaningful act of homoerotically cathected male violence. In these sequences and throughout the film, the display of phallic noses, dildos and large not-so-delicately-concealed codpieces are present less for the purpose of intimidating women than paradoxically for both intimidating and reassuring men. As if playing on male anxieties about penis size, *Clockwork* announces its own anxieties through its aggressive and insistent portrayal of the penis-as-phallus in a variety of guises and uses (Note that Alex's full name is "Alexander de Large"). *Clockwork* dispenses with the possibility of representing male homoeroticism – and the male subject – outside of violence. Thus, violence as the condition of masculine subjectivity paradoxically destroys and enables both subject and object of desire in one broad representational stroke.

The first of these sequences takes place at the Derelict Casino. The first shot is a close-up of a painted sun from which the camera pans down to a long shot of a gang of men raping a young woman on the casino's stage. She unsuccessfully struggles with them, her cries intermingled with the strains of Rossini's overture to "The Thieving Magpie." Because of the setting, the shot, and the music, the rape scene loses a great deal of its horror and instead becomes a comic spectacle. Alex's voice-over reinforces this distancing by referring to the rape as a "game of the old in-out," with the female victim merely a "weepy young devotchka [girl]." Just as Billy Boy's gang has fully undressed the woman and thrown her on a (conveniently placed) mattress, there is a cut to Alex and his gang at the periphery of the large room. Alex calls out to Billy Boy, insulting him and challenging him to a fight, a challenge that Billy Boy and his gang accept with pleasure. The men fight and Alex's gang successfully beats the rivals.

The filming of the woman's rape as a comedy and its deferral to the exuberant fight between men supports the homoerotic tenor of this sequence. When Alex challenges Billy Boy, the camera follows the woman as she runs offstage and escapes. Prior to this shot, the voice-over and shot-reverse-shot pattern between Alex and Billy Boy's gangs link Alex to the extradiegetic spectator, with the struggling woman as the primary object of both gangs' look. Insofar as the camera follows the woman's escape in this sequence, however, the woman-as-spectacle disappears, leaving only men in her place. Furthermore, the music that accompanies this sequence is an overture, an ironic suggestion that the woman's rape functions as a preamble to the more serious and worthy struggle between men.

Mario Falsetto writes of this sequence:

> The violent, choreographed rumble takes place in a pitlike, ground-levelspace that evokes images of Roman gladiators, contemporary wrestling and other acrobatic movement or sport. . . . The exaggerated, fragmented actions are not only theatrical, but also invoke the idea of fantasy. The sequence has the heightened intensity one might associate with the drug-induced reveries of a teenager raised on movies and comic books.
>
> (p. 60)

This "teenager" is not ungendered; while Falsetto situates this "fantasy" in a particular way, he does so by way of references to icons of male homosexual camp, especially "Roman gladiators." In this scene, Kubrick does not distance the spectator from the violence but rather invests the violence with vitality and spirit. When Alex challenges Billy Boy, he taunts "Come and get one in the yarbles [balls] – If you *have* any yarbles." Billy Boy responds "Let's get her, boys." This feminine reference to Alex and his gang signals the homoerotic overtones of the subsequent fight. Although the attempted rape is farcical, the fight scene is represented as comparatively more sexual and phallic, the strains of Rossini swelling in loudness as the fight intensifies. The fight montage concludes when Alex and each member of his gang pair off with Billy Boy and his men. In a long shot, Billy Boy and gang lie in a row on the ground, writhing in pain, while Alex and each of his men beat them with the canes they held at the beginning of the fight. In a close-up of Alex repeatedly beating one of them, the angle of the shot, Alex's cries, and the obvious pleasure he takes from the event imply that the blows could be read as a form of penetration.

Although the second attack is on a heterosexual couple, the homoerotic overtones are no less striking. In the second attack, Alex orchestrates and performs the violence against the writer, Mr. Alexander, and his (significantly) unnamed wife. Upon gaining entrance to their "HOME," Alex beats Mr. Alexander, destroys his bookshelves and written work, and methodically prepares to rape Mr. Alexander's wife – all while singing Gene Kelly's signature, "Singin' in the Rain." Several congruences between the previous brawl and this apparently more calculated and sadistic attack inform this sequence. Alex's staging of Mrs. Alexander's rape parallels Billy Boy's attempted gang rape, which occurs on a literal stage. In this rape, however, Alex moves from the position of spectator to solo performer. He forces Mr. Alexander into the spectatorial position, a shift illustrated through several close-ups of the tormented Mr. Alexander. Just prior to the sequence's conclusion, Alex sneers at Mr. Alexander, saying, "Viddy [look] well, little brother, viddy well." As in the previous attempted rape, the woman and her experience are not considered important. Alex forces Mr. Alexander to witness – and indeed, *experience* – the rape-as-violation and emasculating appropriation.

Clearly, Oedipal overtones structure this rape scene – a reverse restaging of the primal scene, in which the father is forced to watch the son rape the wife/mother (Nelson, p. 154). Other parallels structure a relation between the two men in addition to the similarity in names. The three shots of a bound and gagged Mr. Alexander, suffering over the spectacle of his wife's rape (which we as spectators do *not* see) foreshadow Alex strapped and bound to the chair during his Ludovico treatments or even Alex trapped by Mr. Alexander and forced to listen to the nausea-inducing Beethoven's Ninth Symphony. The actor who plays Mr. Alexander, Patrick Magee, adds an extradiegetic reference to this and the later HOME sequence as well: Magee played Sade in Peter Brook's 1967 film, *Marat/Sade* (Falsetto, p. 156). Ironically, Magee as Mr. Alexander now occupies a masochistic role. This reversal and the homoerotic tenor of the sequence suggest that *Clockwork* relies on sadomasochism in order to represent and disavow male homoeroticism. This particular sadomasochistic scene relies on Mrs. Alexander as the site upon which the violence may take place and gain significance *for the two men* – albeit not for the spectator since the sequence ends just as the rape is about to begin.

The last attempted rape/attack sequence arguably has the most overt sexual content of the three. Here, Alex fights with the Cat Lady in her home and murders her with a penis-shaped art object. She has many works of art depicting sadomasochistic and lesbian sex; perhaps this is the female subject's decorative equivalent of the Korova Milkbar furnishings. Rather than focus on this specific sequence, I want to look at the two events that frame the Cat Lady's murder. This murder (signified by a cartoonish image of a vagina dentata) serves as both prelude to and an outcome of homosocial violence. Through slow motion filming, homosocial violence is invested with more emotion and eroticism than Alex's mock display of physical prowess at the Cat Lady's farm.

Prior to the murder, the gang comes to Alex's flat to complain of his dictatorial style. The sequence takes place in the lobby, which has a large, elaborate wall mural depicting Christ against an extensive biblical tableau. The mural includes only one female figure among a sea of male ones, and the tableau is highly homoerotic; notably, sexual graffiti defaces the mural and all the male figures are muscular and scantily clad. Apart from sexually graphic phrases, the graffiti includes penises and arrows drawn to suggest male homosexual and sodomitical sex scenes. Perhaps most provocatively, Christ, the centerpiece of the mural, has been redrawn with an erection. Set against this backdrop, the showdown clearly acquires a homosexual subtext.

In this sequence, Dim is shot in low angle against the mural as he taunts Alex. Georgie stands behind Dim and leans against the chair, occasionally rocking it: his position alludes to sodomy because of the backdrop, the graffiti, and Georgie's visibly large codpiece. Alex explains that he did not go to the Korova because he "had a pain in the gulliver [head]." Dim responds sarcastically: "Sorry about the pain. Using the gulliver too much, then, eh? Giving orders and discipline, perhaps. Are you sure the pain is gone? Are you sure you wouldn't be happier in bed?" Dim's speech links several discourses operating in the film. Just prior to this scene, Alex picks up two women and has sex with them in his room, another comical heterosexual sex scene, shot in fast motion to the *William Tell* Overture and another reference to heterosexual sex as an overture or diversion. Because of this preceding scene, Dim's reference to "using the gulliver too much" conflates the head with the penis. In his subsequent clause,

12. Alex straddles Dim in his chair.

however, Dim's reference to "orders and discipline" links Alex's sexual acts to his harsh disciplinary control over the gang. As the leader, Alex gets the most out of the gang's exploits, both sexually and financially. Georgie and Dim argue for more of the "big, big, big money" that they feel Alex is hoarding, telling Alex that he "thinks like a little child" and that they want "a man's size" portion. This conflation of discourses surrounding sex, discipline, and money metonymically links the head and penis to the phallus.

Apart from the language, the sexual overtones of this homosocial rivalry are also represented visually. Alex agrees to the gang's demands while straddling Dim in his chair, occasionally patting and touching his shoulders and face [Fig. 12]. Medium-long shots against the mural are interspersed with close-ups of Georgie, Dim, and Alex, creating a stifling, rivalrous intimacy. The gang's coercion of Alex can be read as a seduction, in which sex, discipline, and money are equated. By the end of the scene, one wonders just what "pretty polly" really is and whether it may not be about women at all.

Alex retaliates against this "seduction" at the Flatblock Marina in an extended sequence of slow-motion violence against Dim and Georgie. Through a voice-over, Alex condemns Georgie and Dim bitterly, concluding that "thinking is for the gloopy [stupid] ones, and the omni [smart] ones use inspiration and what Bog [God] sends." Then, Alex hits them with his pole and kicks them in the crotch, knocking them into the water. As he bends down to assist Dim out of the water, he gashes Dim's hand with a hidden knife. Although this sequence is shot in slow motion, the vitality and music echo the homoerotic struggle with Billy Boy's gang. The rampant castration imagery is represented with an almost religious meaningfulness: Alex specifically attacks the men's penises, slowly slices Dim's hand, and rivulets of faux blood stream down Dim's suspenders.

Although this violence temporarily reinstalls Alex as leader of the gang and they proceed to follow Georgie's plan for attacking the Cat Lady, Alex's revenge proves to be his undoing. The post-murder scene marks one of the few moments in the film that does not present violence from Alex's point of view. As Alex exits the Cat Lady's farm, there is a cut to a close-up of a milk bottle, then a fast track back that reveals Dim holding it behind his back. Alex comes face to face with Dim, and the two men are centered in the frame. There is a cut to a profile two shot of them and much as Alex surprised Dim with the knife, Dim now gashes Alex in slow motion. The impact of the bottle breaking sprays milk on Alex in slow motion, his long phallic nose drooping at his chest. As Alex falls to the ground writhing in pain and crying, his droogs laugh at him and run away.

Alex's comeuppance threatens an incestuous deformation of the homosocial order. The film exposes the paradox of this social order by revealing that the homosocial relies upon and is undone by its erotic, violent structure. This realm ultimately pays little attention to arbitrary boundaries and divisions, such as different gangs. This final set of sequences is in some ways the film's most disturbing because it dispenses with the other – women, older men, intellectuals, or the rival gang – and situates the violence within the space that was supposedly safe.

"THE PRISONERS ENJOY THEIR SO-CALLED PUNISHMENT": LUDOVICO TREATMENT AND A RETURN "HOME"

In the second half of *A Clockwork Orange*, Alex is isolated, punished, and physically and psychologically tortured during and after the

Ludovico treatment. The trials Alex experiences in the second half continue the agonistic male homoeroticism deflected only by the film's distantiation and irony. The primary difference between the first and second parts of the film is Alex's overt failure at mastery in the latter, a failure that situates Alex – and, by extension, spectators – in a masochistic position.

I now want to turn to two sets of encounters in the second half of the film – the Ludovico treatment and the second HOME sequence – in order to explore the agonistic and anxious construction of masculinity within a homosocial realm. I will conclude with an analysis of the ending that challenges the celebratory resolution of *Clockwork*'s anxieties and conflicts over masculinity. Its ending must be read retroactively against the preceding enunciation and disavowal of a homoerotic masculinity, one that masquerades (in both the film and many critical analyses) as "humanity."

The minister who chooses Alex for the Ludovico treatment states that Alex is "enterprising, aggressive, outgoing, young, bold, and vicious" and, therefore, "perfect" for the program. Synonyms not only for the film's constructions of masculinity, these characteristics also reflect the broader cinematic constructions of masculinity as a psychic space that shapes the world. While "vicious" may not seem to constitute an ideal characteristic for a *cinematic* male subject, one need only look at some of the most popular Hollywood genres – westerns, gangster/action films, film noir, war films – to see how often a vicious masculinity is rewarded for its propensity toward aggression and violence. *Clockwork* demonstrates the arbitrary hypocrisy of assigning moral value to certain representations of violence. Alex has all the characteristics of a hero but also an arbitrarily defined morality and mercenary sense of self-interest. Consequently, this emphasis forces spectators to focus on the thrill (and trauma) of violence as the source of the self. In order to sustain this edification of Alex's *male* self, however, the film continually must repeat and reexperience the representation of homosocial violence in a variety of sites and forms, and this repetition exacerbates more than alleviates concerns over masculinity's stability.

Thus, that the film should employ the cinematic realm as the site for Alex's "treatment" is no coincidence: its link between masculine subjectivity and an erotics of violence occurs consistently in theatrical performative spaces. The Ludovico treatment sequences, however, do more than link spectatorship, passivity, and a desire to be victimized through one's identifications with on-screen subjects: they also deconstruct the safe distinctions between audience and image. In both scenes of Alex's strait-jacketed spectatorship, a series of people remain visible in the long, deep-focus shot of the theater. Alex sits in the front of the theater, the ostensible audience for the film, but he is also the object of the doctors' gaze. Furthermore, the physical effects of the films on Alex mirror the objectification of Alex-as-spectacle. Although Alex remains the subject of the narrative through his point of view shots and voice overs, shots of the ill and horrified Alex, begging for the images and nausea to stop, are interspersed throughout. This shot-reverse-shot pattern, in combination with the double assault on Alex from the doctors and the film's "gaze," place the extradiegetic spectator in a painfully split position of identification.

In each of the two screenings-as-treatment sequences, both Dr. Brodsky and Dr. Brannon ignore Alex's demands and instead politely issue their own: "You must take your chance, boy. The choice has been all yours. You really must leave it to us, but be cheerful about it." That these three sentiments contradict each other is obvious. That they also illustrate the contradictions and illusions simultaneously promoted and disavowed by cinema may be less so. Cinema encourages the illusion of participation ("You must take your chance"), agency ("The choice has been all yours"), and yet, paradoxically, absolute immobility and passivity ("You really must leave it to us"). Thus, this set of contradictions perfectly mirrors the paradox of spectatorial identification. Alex is at once both subject and object of the gaze, both active and passive psychic subject, much like the extra – diegetic spectator who experiences the cinematic narrative itself.

Just as the film constructs a split identification with Alex, so does it *gender* processes of cinematic identification – especially when Alex performs his new and "cured" identity for an assembled crowd of political, prison, and medical officials. This sequence deconstructs the binary opposition between audience and image with even greater force, partly because the intradiegetic filmic image has been replaced with Alex, a real human being. Again, Alex occupies the space of both subject of the narrative and object of the gaze. The ambiguity

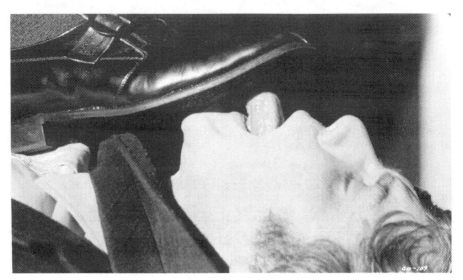

13. A "reformed" Alex licks the shoe of his tormentor.

of his role is evident from the first shot of the sequence – a long, wide-angle, deep focus shot of the theater from the side, with the center of the frame dividing the spectators from the stage. Alex is led into this space and becomes the sole figure on stage, standing silently and somewhat awkwardly until there is a cut to the Minister, who narrates the action.

Alex performs these diegetic scenes somewhat unintentionally. The man and woman who perform with him, however, are clearly aware of their roles as actors in the drama, as evidenced by the pleasure with which they perform and respond to the audience's applause. In this sequence, several shots of Alex on stage are intercut with the prison guard observing him. The guard's differing reactions to Alex's performance both parallel and oppose extradiegetic spectatorial responses. He both takes pleasure in watching Alex lick the man's boot [Fig. 13] and is by turns horrified and astonished by Alex's passivity and nausea in front of the immobile, seminaked woman. The theatricality of the scenes, as well as the split between Alex as object of the diegetic audience's gaze and subject of the voice-over, both reinforce and undermine the film's distancing effects.

The Ludovico sequences also highlight the misogynistic ambivalence toward women. First, while Dr. Brodsky, a man, is in charge of

Alex's treatment, the only doctor shown directly caring for Alex is Dr. Brannon, a stern woman. In one scene, Dr. Brannon enigmatically and menacingly explains to Alex that he feels sick during the films because he is getting better. At this point there is a cut from a low angle close-up of her to the second set of film screenings, the first shot of which foregrounds Hitler and his troops. Although she does not ultimately control Alex's treatment as fully as Brodsky does, the matched cut suggests she does by linking her to Hitler.

Another instance of ambivalence toward women occurs when Alex first experiences nausea during the films. This reaction occurs when the film shows several male gang members raping a woman. The image of gang rape itself, ironically, is not represented as tragic; Alex's horror in being horrified by it is. These rape scene images parallel Billy Boy and his gang's earlier attempted rape, a no-less theatrical affair; thus the Ludovico images act out the deferred rape of the film's opening, reinstalling a heterosexual erotics of violence. On closer inspection, however, this representation of a heterosexual erotics of violence does not stabilize so much as amplify the (homo)sexual anxieties circulating in the text. While these images supposedly represent pleasure for a heterosexual-identified male spectator – they offer unencumbered sexual and visual access to the woman's body – they are highly unpleasurable to Alex.

Perhaps the horror that Alex experiences, while undeniably drug-induced, may stem from the film's equation between seeing and being a victim. While *Clockwork* does not flinch at showing violence to women, such violence becomes horrible only when a kinship is set up between the male subject and the female rape victim as object. Such a kinship recurs throughout the film between Alex and raped women. Apart from this scene, there is visual and aural symmetry between Alex crying in pain at the Cat Lady's door and the "weepy young devotchka" at the Derelict Casino, both scenes set to the same music. More strikingly, perhaps, this kinship recurs in the second HOME sequence, in which Mr. Alexander refers to his now-deceased wife and Alex as "victims of the modern age." Although the staged encounter with the seminaked woman in the theater is not a rape scene per se, the horror of the image lies precisely in the feminization of Alex or, conversely, the triumph of the naked (and therefore presumably powerless) woman over the impotent, passive, clothed Alex. The priest's outburst on Alex's lost moral "choice" enunciates this anxiety clearly. Earlier the priest had taken Alex aside, thinking Alex was suffering from the urges of "normal" men "deprived of the company of women" while incarcerated. As they discussed Alex's submission to the Ludovico treatment, the priest had said that "when a man cannot choose, he ceases to be a man." One wonders then, whether in the cessation of the choice to rape, Alex "becomes" a woman.

The Ludovico treatment demonstrates a link between cinematic spectatorship and violence, exposing a highly gendered process of identification. Male subjectivity, vision, and experience serve as the implicit setting for the exploration of cinematic self-reflexivity. The more *Clockwork* pursues a stable division between men and women, however, the more clearly it eroticizes the homosocial. The homosocial realm, eroticized through violence, replicates a pseudo-heterosexual division from within. Anxieties over what it means to be a man in the landscape of *Clockwork* result in Alex repeatedly being tested, tortured, beaten, and reformed. Such recurring attempts to sustain an oppositional and therefore well-defined masculinity, however, ultimately destabilize the binary opposition of (hetero)sexual difference itself. In this sense, the film's deconstruction of the distance between audience and image parallels its ambivalent treatment of sexual difference.

Several of these themes I have discussed converge in the second HOME sequence. Visually similar to the first HOME sequence, the second opens with a nearly identical medium close-up of Mr. Alexander (now wheelchair-bound) typing on his electric typewriter when the doorbell rings. As the camera pans to the spot where Mrs. Alexander had sat in the first sequence, a muscular man, Julian, is shown lifting barbells instead. Julian answers the door as she did, but carries a collapsed Alex into the dining room to Mr. Alexander, an act that both echoes and inverts the first HOME sequence [Fig. 14]. Mr. Alexander does not remember Alex until he hears Alex singing "Singin' in the Rain," his horror amplified in a distorted low angle, wide angle-lens shot.

Mr. Alexander proceeds to drug and torment Alex: after the drug-laced wine takes effect, Alex unceremoniously passes out face down in his dinner. Alex awakens and is filled with nausea because of the Beethoven he hears emanating from another room. There is a cut to

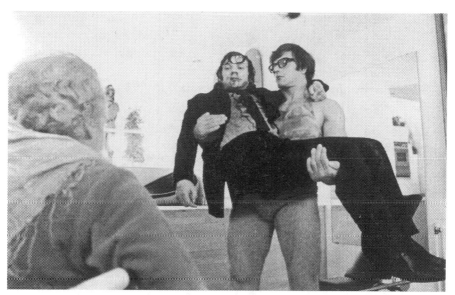

14. Julian (David Prowse) carries the helpless Alex into the dining room.

a close-up of Mr. Alexander, smiling malevolently as the music plays. The camera tracks back from Mr. Alexander to reveal two conspirators and Julian impassively waiting for Alex to jump from the window above them. Eventually Alex does attempt suicide and the fall and imagined point of impact are shot mostly from Alex's point of view.

Throughout this extended sequence, Mr. Alexander recovers authority displaced by the first HOME sequence; Mr. Alexander (or Patrick Magee as Sade?) now takes pleasure in causing Alex's torment. Alex had no explicit reason for his attack, and although Mr. Alexander's revenge provokes pleasure, the inversion of roles suggests a sadomasochistic desire structuring the assault. Furthermore, in the second HOME sequence, the woman is no longer necessary for signifying desire between men. A homoerotic (and possibly homosexual) relation between Julian and Mr. Alexander replaces the heterosexual marriage. Mrs. Alexander, who "used to do everything" for Mr. Alexander, is ultimately less adequate than Julian, given Julian's comparatively greater physical strength. Her *absence* signifies Mr. Alexander's desire for Alex – to be punished with murder – but even her presence in the first sequence suggested an absence of subjectivity. In other words, she was there primarily to signify Mr. Alexander's "rape" in the first sequence, not her own. Her appearance in the red, eye-shaped chair of the first sequence suggests she is not terribly distinct from the Korova "women" – decorative objects against which men measure and become themselves.

The intimacy of the dining room, the same room where the rape took place, and the dinner with wine also evoke an ironic seduction scene. Mr. Alexander heightens this ironic eroticism by insisting Alex have more wine and by moving closer to Alex throughout the dinner. Mr. Alexander compares his wife to Alex and ironically concludes that they are similar. Mr. Alexander, however, is now the menace to Alex, his strained cries for Alex to drink more wine akin to Alex's earlier commands to "viddy well." The first HOME sequence involved invasion of privacy and violent abuse; this sequence reciprocates and parallels that invasion, albeit more discreetly, by contaminating Alex's body with drugs and forcing him to confess his weakness for Beethoven's Ninth and his suicidal tendencies. Alex's body is ultimately attacked by Mr. Alexander just as Alex had attacked Mrs. Alexander's.

Last, Mr. Alexander's tracking shot, in which he sadistically enjoys Alex's torture against a highly stylized tableau of people merging into the decor, parallels Alex's opening tracking shot. Each tracking shot represents the solitary, erotic pleasure of ultraviolence committed for and against men. Throughout this sequence, Mr. Alexander and Alex emerge as inverse images of each other, an inversion underscored by the now-absent figure of the woman (Strick, p. 46). Mr. Alexander and Alex, however, are more than simply father and son, for they are locked in a sadomasochistic exchange. Each HOME sequence offers a site at which one man draws pleasure not from the woman, but rather from the provocation, display, and refusal to assuage male suffering.

If Alex is unwillingly seduced by Mr. Alexander, a seduction that results in a literal and metaphorical fall, then the film's conclusion can be read in similar ways. The conclusion is not necessarily the unmitigated return of Alex's free will, as represented by the will to choose and commit violence. I would suggest that the end – the "cure" – must be read as an ironic and tenuous extension of masculinity as an agonistic, anxious space. Alex's "cure" cements his entrenchment in the state with more disciplinary and bodily control than when he was trapped in prison or strapped in the spectatorial position during the Ludovico treatments. Although the Minister obsequiously seeks Alex's support for political ends and offers Alex material rewards, this support is tenuous. The government can provide Alex "protection" only when in political favor; moreover, given the ease with which "public opinion can be swayed," one wonders how secure Alex's position of material and psychological comfort ultimately may be.

Alex and the Minister's "arrangement" also represents Alex's entrapment in the role of the spectacle (quite literally, given his body cast). His identity will now be constructed through someone else's lens – both literally, given the multiple photographers facing the camera, and metaphorically, by his hypocritical but highly powerful new father figure. The exuberant conclusion of Beethoven, roses, photographers, and Alex's wrestling fantasy may seem the film's ultimate celebration of Alex, but even this fanfare must be read ironically. The narrative recuperates Alex's mastery through recourse to an elaborate fantasy scenario, but how masterful can this recuperation be when the final image must revert to such a surreal, subjective space? Amid the din of the press and the image of the Minister tightly holding his "new friend," Alex is as psychically restrained in the role of spectacle as he is physically restrained in the space of his own body. The final fantasy deflects from the impending force of the state and its disciplinary regimes, but eventually this force will encroach on the space of Alex's own body and desires – unless he knows how to perform.

CONCLUSION

Thomas Elsaesser, in a reading of "Singin' in the Rain" in the first HOME sequence, goes beyond the obvious self-reflexive and Oedipal emphases of the scene and alludes to some of the paradoxes and pleasures I have outlined in my reading:

> [This] scene delves deeply into the nature of cinematic participation and the latent aggression which it can mobilize with impunity: what happens is that before one's eyes an act of brutal violence and sadism is fitted over and made to 'rhyme' with a musical number connoting a fancy-free assertion of erotic longing and vitalist *joie de vivre*. Kubrick is able to exploit the undefined, polyvalent nature of the emotion which the moving image generates, by running, as it

were, two parallel cinematic contexts along the same track, or rather short-circuiting two lines, both charged with emotional energy.

(p. 181)

The image of two parallel tracks running in opposite directions to produce a third, unexpected effect captures not only the representation of violence in *A Clockwork Orange* but also how gender and sexuality circulate in the film as well. Although Elsaesser does not extrapolate on the specificities of how gender and sexuality may relate to this construction, I see Alex and Mr. Alexander – as spectator and performer, father and son, rival and "spouse" – engaging an elaborate series of dualisms beautifully enacted in and through the reference to "Singin' in the Rain." As Gene Kelly was "ready for love," "love," in Kubrick's cinematic landscape, has become not simply heterosexual rape and violence, but, more radically, a sadomasochistic struggle between men. Alex's voice-overs frequently begin with the address "My brothers," an address that extends the narrative's implicit homoeroticism into a conspiratorial incestuousness that engenders the spectator. This homosocial landscape renders women incidental as subjects, prized only insofar as they signify masculinity's otherness.

Clockwork figures this homosocial realm as an erotic landscape, but this eroticism is as strongly disavowed as it is blatantly represented. While all eroticism is marked by violence in *Clockwork*, male homoeroticism is especially marked, resulting in a homophobic identification of male homoeroticism with sadomasochism. Homosociality, unlike the heterosocial and sexual encounters in the film, provides a psychic and physical space in which to act out philosophical questions of what determines "humanity." That eroticized violence ultimately must reconfigure this space as a deeply divided hierarchy suggests the agonistic and anxious nature of the male psyche. Although one of the effects of this process is certainly an overt visual and thematic misogyny, given the disparate treatment of heterosexual and homoerotic encounters, *Clockwork's* erotics of violence cannot be maintained as a purely *heterosexual* erotics of violence. The violence spills over into the homosocial realm, ironically paralleling, mimicking, and even displacing the heterosexual erotics of violence. The anxiety produced by this lack of relief may be deflected through the film's highly ironic lens, but it is not deflected enough to stabilize the shifting boundaries, identifications, and desires that form and deform the masculine subject.

NOTES

1   Some of these critics include Boyers (pp. 1–6), Daniels (pp. 44–46), Falsetto, Nelson, Samuels (pp. 439–43), Houston and Strick (pp. 62–66), and Walker (pp. 7–53).
2   See Daniels, Elsaesser (pp. 171–200), Moskowitz (pp. 22–24), and Kolker (pp. 78–158), and his essay in this volume.
3   Daniels, Falsetto, Nelson, and Walker briefly discuss gender differences in their respective analyses of *Clockwork*.
4   See Hanson (pp. 37–61), Hark (pp. 151–172), Moore (pp. 39–47), Pursell (pp. 218–25), Reaves (pp. 232–237), Walker (pp. 156–221), and White (pp. 120–144).
5   See Berger, Wallis, and Watson; Cohan and Hark; and *Screen*.
6   Because *Clockwork* does not establish an alternate *female* homosocial field, I designate "male homosocial" as simply "homosocial."
7   The excessive whiteness of this opening tracking shot also signals the film's exclusively white racial economy. Interestingly, the only two living women shown in this first shot are African American and Hispanic: presumably whiteness, like masculinity, is the normative backdrop for an analysis of what constitutes the "human."

BIBLIOGRAPHY

Berger, Maurice, Brian Wallis, and Simon Watson, Eds. *Constructing Masculinity*. New York: Routledge, 1995.

Boyers, Robert. "Kubrick's *A Clockwork Orange*: Some Observations." *Film Heritage* 7.4 (1972): 1–6.

Cohan Steven, and Ina Rae Hark, Eds. *Screening the Male: Exploring Masculinities in Hollywood Cinema*. London: Routledge, 1993.

Daniels, Don. "*A Clockwork Orange*." *Sight and Sound* 42 (1972–73): 44–46.

Elsaesser, Thomas. "Screen Violence: Emotional Structure and Ideological Function in *A Clockwork Orange*," in *Approaches to Popular Culture*. C. W. E. Bigsby, Ed. London: Arnold, 1976: 171–200.

Falsetto, Mario. *Stanley Kubrick: A Narrative and Stylistic Analysis*. Westport; CT: Greenwood, 1994.

Hanson, Ellis. "Technology, Paranoia and the Queer Voice." *Screen* 34 (1993): 137–61.

Hark, Ina Rae. "Animals or Romans: Looking at Masculinity in *Spartacus*." *Screening the Male: Exploring Masculinities in Hollywood Cinema*. Steven Cohan and Ina Rae Hark, Ed. London: Routledge, 1993: 151–72.

Houston, Penelope, and Philip Strick."Interview with Stanley Kubrick." *Sight and Sound* 41 (1972): 62–66.

Kolker, Robert. *A Cinema of Loneliness: Penn, Stone, Kubrick, Scorsese, Spielberg, Altman.* New York: Oxford University Press, Third Edition, 2000: 97–174.

Kubrick, Stanley. *A Clockwork Orange.* New York: Balantine Books, 1972.

Kubrick, Stanley, dir. *A Clockwork Orange.* Warner Bros., 1971.

Moore, Janet. "For Fighting and for Fun: Kubrick's Complicitous Critique in *Full Metal Jacket.*" *The Velvet Light Trap* 31 (1993): 39–47.

Moskowitz, Ken. "Clockwork Violence." *Sight and Sound* 46 (1976–77): 22–24.

Mulvey, Laura. "Visual Pleasure in Narrative Cinema." *Visual and Other Pleasures.* Bloomington: Indiana University Press, 1989: 14–26.

Nelson, Thomas Allen. *Kubrick: Inside a Film Artist's Maze.* Bloomington: Indiana University Press, 2000.

Pursell, Michael. "*Full Metal Jacket*: The Unraveling of Patriarchy." *Literature/Film Quarterly* 16 (1988): 218–25.

Reaves, Gerri. "From Hasford's *The Short Timers* to Kubrick's *Full Metal Jacket*: The Fracturing of Identification." *Literature/Film Quarterly* 16 (1988): 232–37.

Samuels, Charles Thomas. "The Context of *A Clockwork Orange.*" *American Scholar* 41 (1972): 439–43.

Screen. The Sexual Subject: A Screen Reader in Sexuality. London: Routledge, 1992.

Sedgwick, Eve Kosofsky. *Between Men: English Literature and Male Homosocial Desire.* New York: Columbia University Press, 1985.

Strick, Philip. "Kubrick's Horrorshow." *Sight and Sound* 41 (1971–72): 44–46.

Walker, Alexander. *Stanley Kubrick Directs.* New York: Harcourt, 1971.

White, Susan. "Male Bonding, Hollywood Orientalism, and the Repression of the Feminine in Kubrick's *Full Metal Jacket.*" *Arizona Quarterly* 44 (1988): 120–44.

4 Stanley Kubrick and the Art Cinema

With *A Clockwork Orange* Stanley Kubrick signaled a new direction for art cinema even as he solidified his position among contemporary auteurs. Although Kubrick has never claimed that he was shifting paradigms for the art film, *A Clockwork Orange* raises crucial questions about how this twist in tradition ought to be understood. By basing his film on the Joycean text of Anthony Burgess's novel, and by emphasizing the book's more nihilistic elements, Kubrick made a film that shared the vision of the "art literature" of high modernism but had little in common with the art cinema of previous decades. The most admired films of Bergman, Kurosawa, Fellini, Truffaut, and the rest took large helpings of inspiration from the Realist novel of the nineteenth century or, as David Bordwell has more specifically suggested, from the works of Chekhov (p. 207). But *A Clockwork Orange* seems to draw upon writers such as Vladimir Nabokov, Bertolt Brecht, and Peter Weiss, as well as Samuel Beckett, who had won the Nobel Prize in 1969 when Kubrick's film was beginning to take shape in the director's mind. As in *Waiting for Godot*, there is nothing to be done in the dystopian future of *A Clockwork Orange*, in spite of the elaborate experiments in social engineering. In an additional departure from the traditions of the art cinema, the bleak, tragicomic vision of *A Clockwork Orange* was dressed up with styles of acting and cinematic violence that were anything but Chekhovian. The film's music, however, suggests that Kubrick was also looking for a more conventional way to associate his film with art.

In her contribution to this volume, Janet Staiger has conducted a thorough archeology of debates in the popular press about the film's politics and its status as a work of art. Not surprisingly, these debates raised issues that were well known from earlier struggles to publish *Ulysses* in the United States and Britain. Like *Ulysses, A Clockwork Orange* can be read as a modernist work because of stylistic flourishes and its biting, often violent humor, some of which struck people as offensive or dangerous. Kubrick's film also has modernist credentials in its harsh critique of contemporary society and the conformism demanded by the welfare state. While social conservatives were most upset about the film's violence and nudity, political leftists were more likely to object to how *A Clockwork Orange* portrayed the future of British socialism. Although the aesthetic and the political in *A Clockwork Orange* offended different groups in different ways, these two aspects of the film might be read as complementary rather than contradictory. Both the aesthetic and political dimensions of Kubrick's critique stem from his rejection of systemic mores and their replacement by individualist, seemingly nihilistic visions. As we will argue later, a similar movement toward iconoclastic individualism is found most strikingly in the modernist literary text par excellence, Joyce's *A Portrait of the Artist as a Young Man* (1916).

David Bordwell's *Narration in the Fiction Film* helps locate *A Clockwork Orange* within the discourses of the art cinema. In a chapter on narration in the art film, Bordwell has assembled the following list to define the art cinema: a "goal-bereft protagonist," an "episodic format," a "central boundary situation," and "spatiotemporal 'expressive' effects" as well as self-referentiality (p. 209). In lacking the goals to which the heroes of conventional genre films usually aspire, Alex (Malcolm McDowell), the protagonist of *A Clockwork Orange*, bears some resemblance to the main characters in films such as *L'Avventura, La Dolce Vita, Jules and Jim, The Passenger, Darling, Young Törless*, and various others. By "episodic format," Bordwell means the kinship of art films to "picturesque and processional forms" and a pattern of "coincidence to suggest the workings of an impersonal and unknown causality" (p. 206). The highly symmetrical progression of Alex's story in *A Clockwork Orange* fits this tradition well; almost everyone who survives Alex's attacks in the opening

15. Stark backlighting, typical of the "spatiotemporal expressive effects" of the art cinema.

moments of the film reappears to torment him at the end with an inevitability that violates the narrative credibility of conventional Realist fiction.

Furthermore, like the main characters in many art films, Alex faces what Bordwell calls "a boundary situation," in which he must decide how to live in a world that makes real change impossible. And although many of the "spatiotemporal effects" of *A Clockwork Orange* have become clichés in the years since the film's release, Kubrick appropriated expressionist techniques in, for example, the stark backlighting of the early scene in which Little Alex and his droogs first encounter the singing tramp [Fig. 15] as well as in the jerky camera and rapid montage of images when Alex smashes the face of the Cat Lady.[1] Finally, like many art films, *A Clockwork Orange* refers both to its director's other films and to the cinema itself.[2] With its allusion to Gene Kelly performing "Singin' in the Rain," its several clips lifted directly from earlier movies, and the clearly visible soundtrack album for *2001: A Space Odyssey* (1968) in a music store, Kubrick seeks to place his work among those revered cinematic texts that are self-conscious and self-referential.

Significantly, Bordwell's discussion of "art cinema narration" is confined to the years 1957–1969 when "the ambiguous interaction of objective and subjective realism reached its apogee" (p. 230). The last films he includes in his discussion are *My Night at Maud's*, *The Damned*, and *The Girls*, as well as *If* . . . , the film in which Malcolm McDowell made his debut[3] (pp. 230–231). Working at the very end of this tradition, Kubrick was perhaps seeking to *reinvent* the art cinema with *A Clockwork Orange*, most prominently with the film's music and its depiction of violence. The sensation of shock, so important to the avant-garde and modernism from Surrealism to the Nouveau Roman – both in cinema and in the other arts – is an integral part of Kubrick's project, even as he foregrounds the music of High Romanticism. But for all its shocking violence and classical music, the film presents a reactionary nihilism along with its aestheticism.

ALEX AND STEPHEN DEDALUS

The Grand Guignol aspects of *A Clockwork Orange* that unnerved many viewers were not unprecedented. Critics had complained loudly about the violence in *Bonnie and Clyde* (1967), while *The Wild Bunch* (1969) was recognized for creating a poetics of blood spurting. But by 1972, few directors had gone as far as Kubrick in aestheticizing violence, both as choreographed spectacle and as closely observed suffering. The sociopathic nature of the hero in *A Clockwork Orange* was not new either. The American cinema has always held a special place for antisocial characters. What Robert B. Ray has called the "outlaw hero" of "real and disguised Westerns" has almost always exhibited a pathological side. Directors such as Hawks and Ford clearly sensed this when they asked John Wayne to play possessed characters in *Red River* (1948) and *The Searchers* (1956). Later, directors such as Milos Forman and Martin Scorsese made the psychopathology of their heroes even more explicit in films such as *One Flew Over the Cuckoo's Nest* (1975) and *Taxi Driver* (1976). One can argue that MacMurphy (Jack Nicholson) in *One Flew* distinguishes himself by standing up for Billy Bibbit (Brad Dourif) and that Travis Bickle (Robert De Niro) succeeds in returning Iris (Jodie Foster) to her parents. For some audiences, these fascinating psychopaths were not substantially different from the characters that had once been played by Wayne, Gable, and Bogart in film after film during Hollywood's Classical period. Although Alex repels the viewer in ways that are not entirely typical of the old Hollywood, especially in the graphic sexual violence he enjoys, he also bears resemblances to at least one character from a defining modernist text who both fascinated and repelled readers.

A brief comparison with Joyce's *Portrait* suggests that both Kubrick and Joyce embrace the modernist paradigm of artist-as-hero, in spite of their rejections of Chekhovian realism. For both, the artist-hero rejects older systems of belief but never challenges the need for such a system. The hero's consciousness functions as the arbiter of society and as the only index of change. In *Portrait*, Stephen Dedalus anticipates Kubrick's Alex by rebelling against country and patriotism ("Ireland is a sow that eats her farrow" [p. 220] and "A race of clodhoppers" [p. 272]). Earlier in the novel Stephen's friend Temple makes a remark, ostensibly about Jean-Jacques Rousseau, but implicitly a judgment on Stephen Dedalus: "He's the only man I see in this institution that has an individual mind" (p. 217). The conjunction of the terms "institution" and "individual" establishes the basic choices for the soon-to-be-exiled Stephen.

Alex, too, in *A Clockwork Orange* has a cynical view of his parents, clearly rejecting their jobs, their care, and their aesthetics. He rightly sees the dreariness of their lives as sterile, their intake of sleeping pills as an easy escape from the world. He turns an equally jaundiced eye on politician-fathers of the left (the Marxist writer F. Alexander, the initial standing perhaps for "father of" Alexander, or Alex) and of the right (the Minister for the Interior, who hand-feeds Alex at the end of the film). The institutions of the family, industry, and politics are seen as corrupt and unsatisfying. In *Portrait*, Stephen hates Catholicism, more specifically those who administer it ("a priestridden race"), while Alex cynically exploits the opportunity to "save his soul" in prison by manipulating the chaplain and by appropriating his sermons for lubricious daydreams. Burgess and Kubrick portray religion more ambiguously by making the chaplain the only character who speaks up against the experiment in social engineering that produces the "reformed" Alex, killing his violence and his freedom to choose. Both Stephen and Alex reject home, friendship, church, and conventional narratives of sex only in order to exalt themselves and their antisocial visions of life. At the end of *Portrait*, Stephen Dedalus recites his mantra, *non serviam*, telling Cranly, "I will not serve that in which I no longer believe whether it call itself my home, my fatherland or my church" (p. 268). Later, in a paean to self-begetting, he hails his true father, Daedalus: "Old father, old artificer, stand me now and ever in good stead" (p. 271). The artifice of the re-productive model that he chooses refers both to art and to his choice, which is unnatural. Similarly, at the end of *A Clockwork Orange* Alex chooses neither his biological father, nor the Marxists who want to "rescue" him, nor the politician-father who spoon-feeds him. Instead he chooses Beethoven. The parents both Alex and Stephen hail re-side in their imagination and, more importantly, in art. Stephen sees himself as the son of the "old artificer" whose job it is to "Live, to fall, to triumph, to recreate life out of life" (p. 186). Alex's moment of triumph at the end of the film is heralded by Ludwig van's Ninth. His salvation is not at the hands of the politician placing nourishment in his mouth nor in the photographers hailing his rebirth and certainly not in the ambiguous interventions of the pretty young psychologist. He is saved through his restored capacity to enjoy Beethoven and to use the music once again as the soundtrack for his violent pleasures.

Nevertheless, neither Alex nor Stephen take the opportunity of ex-ile or violence to articulate a critique of the institutions themselves. What takes the place of such a critique is the privileging of the in-dividual's mind and his creativity. At the end of *A Clockwork Orange*, Alex's feeding at the hands of the minister is soon replaced by his own private wet dream. Such excessive anti-institutional individualism is as alien to the conventional "outlaw hero" of classical Hollywood as it is to the more passive, aimless protagonist of French New Wave cin-ema. Stephen too exults in his dependence on stealth and cunning. This is escapism, not critique.

It is not just in the superficial similarities of character that the two texts echo each other. Kubrick's style in *A Clockwork Orange* bears similarities to Joyce's free indirect style in *Portrait*. If, as Bordwell claims, the camera in classical Hollywood functions as an invisible omniscient narrator (p. 160), Kubrick departs from tradition by using Alex's first-person narration as what Henry James has called the "cen-ter of consciousness." The exaggerated makeup on his right eye calls attention to Alex's surrogate camera that watches the action around

16. With typical Kubrickian centering, Alex looks out with his camera eye.

him [Fig. 16]. The diction in Joyce's novel regularly follows Stephen's acquisition of language and vocabulary, from the baby talk of the first chapter to the precocious sophomoric style of the "aesthetic theory." Similarly, the audience is allowed little critical distance from Alex's perception of the world. When he rams the penis sculpture into the Cat Lady, the viewer watches it from Alex's perspective, forced to assent in Alex's anger against the snobbery and privilege of an eccentric lady who sees the giant penis as art [Fig. 17].

As critics are fond of pointing out, audiences effectively experience the Ludovico treatment *along with* Alex, whose camera eyes are not allowed to flinch at what he sees. And Kubrick has described how he literally threw a running camera out of a window to capture Alex's point of view when he attempts suicide by defenestration at the writer's home (Strick and Houston pp. 64–65). When Alex is absent, his voice-over explains the *mala fide* nature of other people's actions to us, as when his droogs plan to betray him. But when Alex is in the dark, for example when the writer plans to torture him with the *Ninth*, the audience share's Alex's ignorance of the writer's plans. This mode of narration subverts the classical style by blurring the usual distance between the spectator and protagonist-narrator and by encouraging unusually close identification with an unlikely hero. The art cinema narration of the 1950s and 1960s, by contrast, allows

17. Kubrick and his camera stand in for the Cat Lady.

the viewer a much greater distance – even an ironic distance – from the protagonists. The *succès de scandale* enjoyed by *A Clockwork Orange* upon its release was only partially the result of the violence and the graphic rape scene. Equally significant was the film's unrelenting insistence that the audience share the protagonist/narrator's point of view, including his tastes in music.

ROSSINI, PURCELL, AND LUDWIG VAN

The musical score of *A Clockwork Orange* inscribes the aesthetic ideals of Romanticism and Modernism, rejecting the more conventional "invisible" and "inaudible" music that Claudia Gorbman has identified as standard practice in classical cinema. Stanley Kubrick can claim a prominent place in film music history if only for his decision to release *2001: A Odyssey* (1968) with the "temp track" of music by Richard Strauss, Johann Strauss, Aram Khachaturian, and György Ligeti. According to Vincent LoBrutto's biography of Kubrick, the director violated the usual relationship between director and composer by not allowing Alex North to see any part of *2001* while he was under contract to write the music for the film (p. 305). Instead, Kubrick gave North the music from the temp track and told him that he wanted something along those lines. Kubrick may have made up his mind to use the temp track music even before North was brought into the project. Regardless, Kubrick rejected all the music that North eventually composed, but he neglected to tell North, who arrived at the premier of *2001* expecting to hear his own music (North, n.p.). Like Vladimir Nabokov, who published his *Lolita* screenplay after Kubrick discarded it, North made plans to release his rejected score on CD. In 1991, however, North died before the music was actually recorded and released.

Long before he made the revolutionary decision to go with the temp track for *2001*, Kubrick was extremely sensitive to the importance of music for films. His two short subjects for RKO-Pathé from 1951, *Day of the Fight* and *Flying Padre*, were released with no dialogue and very little diegetic sound. These first two items in the Kubrick filmography are carried almost exclusively by disembodied narration, but the films' images are bathed in music – and not just any music. Even though he was working on the tiniest of budgets, Kubrick refused to follow the standard RKO-Pathé practice of using canned music with the images for his first film, *Day of the Fight*. He happened to know Gerald Fried, who was at that time an oboe player and a student at Juilliard living in the Bronx in the same neighborhood as Kubrick.

Fried had no experience writing music, but as he has suggested in his interviews, he was the only musician that Kubrick knew at the time (LoBrutto p. 67). Kubrick was so impressed with what Fried eventually accomplished with his score for *Day of the Fight* that he hired Fried to write music for his first four full-length films, *Fear and Desire* (1953), *Killer's Kiss* (1955), *The Killing* (1956), and *Paths of Glory* (1957). Working comfortably within the neo-romantic traditions of the classical Hollywood score, Fried would later compose scores for films such as *The Killing of Sister George* (1968), *Soylent Green* (1973), and *Nine to Five* (1980). Fried's love theme for Kubrick's *Killer's Kiss* (1955) and his use of jazz piano to mark the sexuality of Marie Windsor in *The Killing* (1956) are entirely consistent with the basic categories for extradiegetic music in Hollywood films as identified by Gorbman.

In Kubrick's *Paths of Glory* (1957), his final collaboration with Gerald Fried, the soundtrack functions differently. Fried scored a rousing version of "La Marseillaise" for the opening credits, but the only music he composed specifically for the film plays early on behind three soldiers as they crawl out of their trenches into No Man's Land. These extradiegetic sounds are created entirely by percussion instruments. (Later, when the three soldiers are led to their death before the firing squad, we again hear a Fried composition exclusively for percussion, but this time the music is diegetic – we actually see the drummers.) Unlike the music in Kubrick's earlier films, the other diegetic music in *Paths of Glory* is more likely to be ironic, especially the Johann Strauss waltz, "Artists' Life," which plays loudly on the soundtrack after almost thirty minutes of film *without* any music at all. Emphasizing the grotesque disparity between the life of high-ranking officers and the fate of the three soldiers arbitrarily condemned to death, the music bursts onto the soundtrack as Kirk Douglas arrives at a lavish officers' party in hopes of making one final appeal for the lives of the three men. Gorbman has called this kind of music "anempathic": the light-hearted music of Strauss plays on, oblivious to what the central character is feeling, not to mention the death toll that supports the good life led by the officers.

Strauss's music makes the palatial quarters of the French generals even more ghastly. One of Kubrick's obsessions, and one of his great achievements as a filmmaker, is his creation of magnificent interiors that become horrifying once we realize that they support what are essentially killing machines. The Overlook Hotel in *The Shining* is the most obvious example, but consider also Quilty's mansion in *Lolita*, the War Room in *Dr. Strangelove*, the high-tech interior of the Jupiter space ship in *2001*, and the enormous bathroom in Ziegler's mansion in *Eyes Wide Shut*. The lethal system that supports these interiors is often made more appalling by a musical score that seems oblivious to what they represent.

Paths of Glory also presents an elegant summary of Kubrick's musical practice. The percussive compositions of Gerald Fried are an excellent example of the unconventional, ominous music Kubrick regularly used to create suspense, while the Strauss waltz is typical of the more accessible, often frivolous, music that Kubrick frequently attached to his most horrifying scenes. Like the ballroom scene with the Strauss waltz, the last moments of music in *Paths of Glory* clash purposefully with what the audience has just seen. As the film draws to an end, a captured German woman is forced to sing to a large group of French soldiers who initially mock her but eventually share a cathartic moment as they tearfully join her in song. Played by Christiane Harlan (who would eventually marry Kubrick and who was still married to him when he died), the terrified German woman sings "The Faithful Hussar." With lyrics that both romanticize and satirize the life of a soldier, the song was popular among German troops during World War I:

Es war einmal ein treuer Husar,
der liebt sein Mädchen ein ganzes Jahr,
ein ganzes Jahr und noch viel mehr,
die Liebe nahm kein Ende mehr.
Und als man ihm die Botschaft bracht,
dass sein Herzliebchen im Sterben lag,
da liess er all sein Hab und Gut
und eilte seinem Herzliebchen zu.
"Ach bitte, Mutter, bring ein Licht,"
mein Liebchen stirbt, ich seh es nicht,"
das war fürwahr ein treuer Hussar,
der liebt sein Mädchen ein ganzes Jahr.

(There was a faithful Hussar
who loved a girl for a whole year
a whole year and even much longer,
their love never ended.
And when he got the message
that his sweetheart was dying,
he left all his belongings behind
and hurried to see his sweetheart.
Please, mother, bring a light,
"my beloved is dying, I won't see her anymore."
He was, indeed, a faithful Hussar,
who loved his woman for a whole year.)

In *Paths of Glory*, "The Faithful Hussar" is performed after the execution of three innocent men and is revealed to be a sham even as it works its magic on the surviving soldiers. Since the men only hum the tune, it is possible that they do not understand the lyrics, which wryly suggest that all soldiers, with the single exception of the one *treuer Hussar*, are free spirits who enjoy multiple conquests with the ladies. Although the music may superficially seem to unite the French soldiers with a representative of the enemy, in full context it continues the film's project of debunking the military ideal. Fried's score deepens the irony even further by concluding with a highly militarized orchestral version of "The Faithful Hussar" over the end credits.

After *Paths of Glory*, Kubrick had much less control over *Spartacus* (1960), and much more control over *Lolita* (1962), but both films make similar use of extradiegetic music. Alex North's score for *Spartacus* has a few modernist dissonances, but it departs little from the post-Wagnerian traditions of classical Hollywood. Similarly, Nelson Riddle's jazz- and pop-inflected score for *Lolita* sits comfortably in the background and makes familiar gestures. Both films have highly charged love themes for the most romantic moments. Perhaps because *Lolita* is a much more ironic film, Riddle was not always in on the joke, and the music does not consistently correspond precisely to what takes place on the screen. For example, when James Mason reads the stilted letter in which Shelley Winters declares her love, the music signifies conventional romance in spite of the fact that Mason is laughing out loud at the prose. Nevertheless, Riddle's music is typically Kubrickian in mixing two kinds of music. The childlike, sing-songy Lolita theme is often heard while Humbert and Lolita live out their mockery of life as father and daughter. Later, when Humbert makes his final declaration of love to the pregnant, bespectacled Lolita, Riddle's emotionally turbulent, sub-Rachmaninoff piano concerto rumbles in the background. The piano music promises a climax, and indeed Humbert then goes off to kill Clare Quilty.

Nelson Riddle, at any rate, never again worked with Kubrick. The veteran British composer Laurie Johnson receives credit for the score of Kubrick's next film, *Dr. Strangelove* (1964), but by this time the music has clearly been chosen by the director. If Kubrick managed to slip a few sexual jokes and innuendoes past the censors in *Lolita*, he was especially daring at the opening of *Strangelove* when the sweet orchestral strains of "Try a Little Tenderness" can be heard alongside footage of airplanes copulating. The satire becomes substantially more intense at the film's conclusion when Vera Lynn sings "We'll Meet Again" as hydrogen bombs explode. The only other music in the film further enforces Kubrick's Swiftian project; a solemn version of "When Johnny Comes Marching Home Again" always plays behind scenes on the B-52 bomber commanded by Major Kong (Slim Pickens). *Dr. Strangelove* is unique, we believe, in being the only film in Kubrick's mature work that *only* uses what we might properly call "popular" music. The portentous music function is fulfilled, atypically, by the completely accessible sounds of "When Johnny Comes Marching Home Again."

Dr. Strangelove looks forward to *2001: A Space Odyssey*, another film with soundtrack music that flamboyantly calls attention to itself. No one who has seen *2001* would say that Richard Strauss's *Also Sprach Zarathustra* is "inaudible" as it plays behind the spectacular alignment of earth, moon, and sun. This is Kubrick's typically auspicious music, like Ligeti's *Requiem for Soprano, Mezzo-Soprano, Two Mixed Choirs and Orchestra* that accompanies the discovery of the Monolith by the apemen and the Adagio from the *Gayanne Ballet Suite* by Khachaturian that plays while Gary Lockwood takes his jog through the eerie confines of the spaceship. By contrast, the much more accessible "Blue Danube" of Johann Strauss is the ironic accompaniment to spaceships floating through the cold depths of space.

Although Kubrick asked his audiences to make sense of some unusual signifying practices in the music for *2001*, he probably did not expect them to know who had composed the music or when. Audiences were so accustomed to the Wagnerian traditions of Hollywood music that anyone not familiar with *Also Sprach Zarathustra* probably did not realize that the piece had been composed in 1896. And because music for science fiction films has almost always tended to be dissonant and moody, audiences were even less likely to speculate about who composed the modernist works that play on the soundtrack.

For *A Clockwork Orange*, however, Kubrick chose music that audiences were much more likely to recognize. The most obvious example is "Singin' in the Rain," one of the best known songs from

Hollywood. As the 1974 compilation film *That's Entertainment!* points out, Cliff Edwards, Judy Garland, and Jimmy Durante all performed "Singin' in the Rain" in different MGM films before the release of the film called *Singin' in the Rain* in 1952.[4] In *A Clockwork Orange*, Little Alex performs "Singin' in the Rain" as part of a brutal dance during which he repeatedly groin-kicks the Writer and then rapes the Writer's wife before his eyes. The second time Alex performs the song he is in the bath at the Writer's house. Happy to have found shelter, Alex sings in the spirit of his earlier, carefree personality even as the Writer in the room below begins to realize the identity of his guest. The song is reprised again with a lilting vocal by Gene Kelly as the final credits roll, creating the same kind of ironic effect as "Try a Little Tenderness" at the beginning of *Dr. Strangelove* and "The Faithful Hussar" at the end of *Paths of Glory*. Once again, the upbeat quality of popular music is meant to emphasize rather than to distract us from the horror in the film's events. And of course "Singin' in the Rain" gives an art film effect to *A Clockwork Orange* by referring to an earlier cinematic tradition.

Most of the music in *A Clockwork Orange*, however, comes from a tradition that is even more honored than the one represented by *Singin' in the Rain*. In the event that some audience members need help, the name Beethoven is regularly heard throughout the film. Kubrick also gives the audience numerous representations of the composer's famous face, probably the one image most associated with our culture's notion of a Romantic artist. Thomas Allen Nelson has even suggested that the image of Beethoven staring intently from under a lowered brow is intentionally echoed in the film's first image of Alex's face. (Of course, the purposeful stare from beneath a lowered brow would eventually become a standard Kubrick index for madness. Consider Jack Nicholson in *The Shining*, Vincent D'Onofrio in *Full Metal Jacket*, and even Patrick Magee as the Writer when he last appears in *A Clockwork Orange*.)

But Beethoven is not the only composer the audience is invited to identify. Those of us who were raised on *The Lone Ranger* in the 1950s can recognize Rossini's *William Tell* Overture when Alex takes home the two girls from the record store. Although spectators are not likely to know the other composition by Rossini, the Overture to *Thieving Magpie*, which accompanies the attack by Alex and his mates on a rival gang, the audience probably understands how this ancient piece of classical music is inappropriate to the futuristic mise-en-scène at the same time that it is appropriate to the stylized chore-ography of the fight. The irony is much more heavy-handed than, say, the presence of a Strauss waltz as Kirk Douglas prepares to make his desperate appeal to Adolphe Menjou in *Paths of Glory*. Kubrick probably hoped that the music in *A Clockwork Orange* would ennoble the film by associating it on multiple levels with the traditions of European art music. Significantly, Kubrick also made use of short ex-cerpts from two well-known pieces, Rimsky-Korsakov's *Scheherezade* and Elgar's *Pomp and Circumstance*, so that audiences could congrat-ulate themselves on their knowledge of great music or, to phrase it more cynically, their knowledge of middle-brow orchestral music from the past that is often crassly marketed as "The Greatest Music the World Has Known." In spite of his antiheroic qualities, Alex re-sembles the bourgeois who demands respectful silence at the concert hall, as when he whacks Dim so that he can hear the woman at the bar singing lieder.

Barry Lyndon (1975), Kubrick's first film after *A Clockwork Orange*, is a more conventional art film with a much more extensive ar-ray of classical music by Mozart, Bach, Schubert, Vivaldi, and Han-del. For vernacular music, Kubrick chose songs by composer Sean O'Riada and a number of traditional Irish tunes performed by The Chieftains. According to John Baxter, Kubrick believed that the time had come to create his masterpiece and that *Barry Lyndon* would be "the best British historical film ever" (p. 278). This may explain why Kubrick chose so much venerated music without caring if audiences recognized it. Although some critics would argue that Kubrick achieved his goal and that *Barry Lyndon* is among his great-est works, the film was also his biggest box office failure. As Robert Sklar has argued, the director subsequently learned how to make a more financially successful film, casting the highly bankable Jack Nicholson in *The Shining* (1980) and carefully opening the film at the most propitious moment. *The Shining* has a great deal of difficult, portentous music and at least one example of everyday, popular mu-sic playing against the grain. For example, audiences hear the Adagio from Bartok's *Music for Strings, Percussion, and Celeste* as Danny cau-tiously approaches his father, clairvoyantly suspecting that his father will soon try to kill him. By contrast, the banal theme of the Road Runner cartoon provides an anempathic counterpoint to the desperate situation of mother and son as they sit in front of the television, supposing that Jack has been safely locked away after Wendy stopped his assault with a baseball bat. Significantly, most of the music in *The Shining*, including the Bartok composition, is largely "inaudible" in Gorbman's sense and probably does not impress the casual viewer as substantially different from music in other horror films.

For the suspenseful moments in *Full Metal Jacket* (1987), Kubrick uses a bit of synthesizer music for an eerie, squeaky door effect as when Joker (Matthew Modine) cautiously approaches the sniper girl. Composed by Kubrick's daughter, Vivian (listed in the credits as Abigail Mead), this music functions much like the percussive score for *Paths of Glory*, the *Requiem* by Ligeti in *2001*, and Bartok's music in *The Shining*. But the most memorable music in *Full Metal Jacket* is its assortment of monumentally frivolous recordings from the mid-1960s, including "Woolly Bully," "Chapel of Love," "These Boots are Made for Walkin'," and "Surfin' Bird." Kubrick uses vernacular music both diegetically and extradiegetically throughout *Full Metal Jacket* to remind audiences that the soldiers, many of them still in their teens, are asked to give their own lives and to take the lives of others even though they are still very much a part of the adolescent culture represented by the pop tunes. "Surfin' Bird," for example, erupts on the soundtrack right after a young G.I. guns down several enemy soldiers and then breaks into an innocent, surprised grin. The soundtrack music for most of Hollywood's war movies carries safer sets of meaning. John Williams' Coplandesque score for *Saving Private Ryan* (1998), for example, helps turn it into a conventional combat film about men dying heroically in battle. Imagine what *Saving Private Ryan would* have been if Spielberg had imitated Kubrick and used popular songs from the WWII era such as Kay Kyser's "Three Little Fishes in an Itty Bitty Poo" instead of all those majestic French horns borrowed from Aaron Copland.[5]

In his final film, *Eyes Wide Shut* (1999), the musical choices are usually consistent with Kubrick's established musical practices. For example, the ominous chanting music composed for the film by Jocelyn Pook dominates the soundtrack when the masked Bill Harford (Tom Cruise) first arrives at the orgy on the Long Island estate. When he walks into the large room where the mock court is in session, the music is the starkly struck piano notes from *Musica Ricercata, II* by Kubrick's old favorite, György Ligeti. And later in the film, when Bill enters a coffee shop and sees the newspaper article that leads him to suspect that a woman who saved him the night before has been murdered, the music is from Mozart's *Requiem*. For the more familiar genres of music, Kubrick has chosen recordings by obscure bandleaders Peter Hughes and Victor Silvester, who specialize in what might be called "light" dance music. We hear this kind of music while Bill and Alice (Nicole Kidman) attend the absurdly lavish Christmas party at the Zieglers and later when Bill is at the orgy, assuming incorrectly that he has achieved anonymity. The benign dance music is utterly inappropriate to the menacing worlds in which it is heard, much like the Strauss waltz in *Paths of Glory*.

It is entirely possible that Kubrick died before he had finalized the musical choices for *Eyes Wide Shut*.[6] Nevertheless, if past practice is any indication, Kubrick may have used bits of popular music to undermine the appeal of his two beautiful protagonists. For example, Chris Isaak sings his tepid pop ballad "Baby Did a Bad Bad Thing" while Alice and Bill pose nude in front of a mirror, watching themselves rather than their mates. Kubrick may be placing Isaak's song in the same category as "Surfin' Bird" and "Woolly Bully." At the film's conclusion, the audience hears the *only* piece of Christmas music in a film that is suffused with Christmas cards, Christmas trees, and Christmas greetings. If a perfunctory version of "Jingle Bells" is the music that Kubrick really wanted at the end of *Eyes Wide Shut*, then he may be asking us to find the spectacle of Alice and Bill soullessly shopping for Christmas presents while teaching their daughter to be, like them, a good consumer a bit horrifying.

In *A Clockwork Orange*, Kubrick does retreat from his comfortably familiar "high art" score now and then for the pop music effect that is so distinctive in *Full Metal Jacket* and *Eyes Wide Shut*. When Alex returns home to his family after being discharged from the Ludovico Institute, the apartment is filled with the inane sounds of Erika Elgen's "I Want to Marry a Lighthouse Keeper." The song seems intended to increase our alarm over Alex's rejection by his own parents. The audience is meant to find this scene more upsetting than the violent ballet earlier in the film when bodies are being bludgeoned to the sounds of Rossini's *Thieving Magpie*. These kinds of choices led the critic Jonathan Rosenbaum to refer to *A Clockwork Orange* as "morally repugnant." Certainly, the film is much less progressive than other films by Kubrick, especially in its calculated veneration of high culture and in its ridiculing of attempts to improve human society.

The classical music that is essential to Kubrick's aesthetic project in *A Clockwork Orange* becomes most central when Beethoven's Ninth Symphony is accidentally mixed in with the violence and sexuality that Alex is being conditioned by the Ludovico treatment to reject. Other than the continual abuse from a variety of characters and institutions that the young protagonist suffers throughout the second half of the film, Alex's affection for Beethoven may be his most sympathetic quality. Just as Joyce's Stephen transcends his despised milieu by invoking the figure of Dedalus from classical myth, Alex casts the mythic and classical Beethoven as his ultimate father figure, an idealized patriarch from the Land of Art. During the Ludovico treatment, Alex protests the use of the Turkish March from the Ninth Symphony to accompany the screening of a Nazi procession in *Triumph of the Will*. When he cries out, "It's a sin!", the female scientist cannot understand why he should object to hearing a Beethoven symphony, referring to it only as "the background score." As Peter Rabinowitz points out in his essay in this collection, Anthony Burgess's novel makes a clear connection between masculine violence and the musical traditions surrounding Beethoven: "German music and German atrocities cannot be easily disassociated" (p. 109). In the film, by contrast, the music of the beloved Ludwig van is apparently connected with the Nazi footage only by coincidence. By objecting to this juxtaposition, Alex proves once again that he is the only character in the film with a finely developed aesthetic sense.

The casual manner in which the Ludovico engineers allow the sounds of Beethoven to become another stimulus to Alex's nausea discredits their work from the beginning. The impassioned critique of Alex's conditioning delivered later by the prison chaplain takes on additional moral authority through its association with Beethoven's music. Rather than problematizing the fascination that Beethoven holds for a violent young sociopath, the film allows the German composer to retain his heroic significations. This is especially true of scenes in which Beethoven displaces more traditional idols in Alex's mind. In the early scene when Alex masturbates to Beethoven in bed after a night of "ultraviolence," the camera slowly pans across a chorus line of plastic Jesus figures, who could be kicking in unison to the music and who are rendered meaningless by their inappropriateness. By later objecting to the juxtaposition of Beethoven and Nazi violence, Alex proves once again that he is the only character in the film with independent good taste and thus the only character worth caring about.

Earlier in the film when Alex inserts a cassette recording of Beethoven's Ninth into his stereo system at home, he chooses a version conducted by Herbert von Karajan.[7] But there is another version of the Ninth on the film's soundtrack. Wendy (then Walter) Carlos, who hit the number-one slot on Billboard's classical music charts in 1968 with *Switched-On Bach*, provided Kubrick with some switched-on Beethoven. Working with Robert Moog to make the synthesizer an essential part of musical culture in the 1970s, Carlos invited audiences to hear the stuffy old tones of the European canon in a striking new way. Kubrick almost certainly approved of Carlos's work and was more than happy to bring his music to a large and receptive audience. The director also chose *The William Tell* Overture, *Scheherezade*, and *Pomp and Circumstance* knowing that audiences would feel at home with this music. In addition, Kubrick appropriated Carlos's electrified version of Henry Purcell's *Music for the Funeral of Queen Mary* to create the familiar Kubrickian sense of foreboding, especially at the beginning of *A Clockwork Orange* when the camera closes in on Alex as he looks out from under his brow at the Korova Milkbar.

In spite of Kubrick's use of popularized versions by Carlos, his appropriation of Beethoven is emblematic of the film's troubling embrace of Little Alex over any other character or institution. The musicologist Scott Burnham has traced the development of Beethoven's heroic stature through two centuries of music criticism. He finds a long line of writers who have assigned to Beethoven's music "the highest values of their age, those of freedom and self-determination, as well as the decidedly human (as opposed to godlike or demigod-like) nature of the heroic type" (p. 25). Creating a character who is literally deprived of his "freedom and self-determination," Kubrick would dignify the struggles of Alex by invoking this tradition of the Beethoven myth.

ALEX AND RICHARD III

Perhaps seeking to further legitimate the film's status as art, Kubrick compared Alex to Shakespeare's Richard III (Strick and Houston p. 63). Unlike Shakespeare's character, however, Alex strikes audiences as sympathetic primarily because they are invited to have little or no sympathy for his victims or his victimizers. Consider the soldiers executed in *Paths of Glory*, the sniper girl in *Full Metal Jacket*, and even the apemen struck down by other apemen in *2001*. In every case, the victims are hardly paragons of virtue, but they are treated with more sympathy than, say, the Cat Lady in *A Clockwork Orange*. Like *A Portrait of the Artist as a Young Man*, Kubrick's film portrays a profoundly bankrupt culture. By questioning the basic belief that humans are at some level worth saving, *A Clockwork Orange* refuses the optimistic mythology expressed in mainstream Hollywood as well as in most of the art films of the 1950s through the 1960s. In its pessimism and nihilism, as well as in its rejection of scientific-rationalist models of social progress, the film has much in common with the fiction of Joyce, not to mention much of the "serious" literature of the second half of the twentieth century. Kubrick has not explicitly made this claim, but many of his critics have made it for him. Thomas Allen Nelson, for example, celebrates Kubrick's "aesthetic complexity" in philosophical language:

> An awareness of contingency arises whenever there is a loss of faith in teleological explanations, in the inviolability of institutionalized meaning, in the rational structures of nature or the signifying power of mind and language. Once meaning has lost the authority of inherent design and purpose, we then perceive how many different ways there are to create meaning through the expressive extensions of language and form.
>
> (p. 16)

For Nelson, Kubrick has been exploring the possibilities for action within a fallen world at least since *The Killing*. We would suggest, however, that the director's interest in philosophical issues was developed most flamboyantly in the finale of *2001*, with its climax recalling Teilhard de Chardin.

By contrast, in *A Clockwork Orange*, human perfectibility is a joke, producing Kubrick's most noticeable transformations of the art cinema. One of the most consistent emblems of the art cinema of the 1950s and 1960s was its naturalistic, often self-effacing style of acting, not coincidentally based in the Stanislavskian method that first became codified in productions of Chekhov's plays at the Moscow Art Theatre. Kubrick, who never seemed comfortable with actors from the beginning, moved away from Method acting most prominently when he devoted much of *Lolita* and *Dr. Strangelove* to the improvisations of Peter Sellers.[8] The often brilliant performances of Sellers in *Strangelove* were complemented by the stylized acting of Sterling Hayden, George C. Scott, and Slim Pickens. In *2001*, by contrast, Kubrick gave the most ostentatious acting role to Douglas Rain as the passionless voice of HAL, the computer. In *A Clockwork Orange*, many of the performances are highly stylized, especially the late scenes with Patrick Magee that prompted Pauline Kael to suggest that the actor was auditioning for a future in horror films (P. 52). But the performances of Michael Bates (Chief Guard), Aubrey Morris (Deltoid), and Godfrey Quigley (Prison Chaplain) are just as overdrawn. Kubrick seems to be misanthropically characterizing the human animal as essentially histrionic, tending toward the Bergsonian mechanical. Even Alex's mother is caricatured, dressing in a hideous miniskirt and listening to "I Want to Marry a Lighthouse Keeper" while she rests on the sofa with the young lodger who has replaced Alex.

Rather than allowing Alex to be conventionally redeemed at the end of *A Clockwork Orange*, Kubrick lets Malcolm McDowell engage in his most highly mannered acting in the final scenes, including his forced laughter in the scene with the female psychologist and his exaggerated chewing as the Minister of the Interior feeds him pieces of steak. So striking was Malcolm McDowell's chewing that it earned the distinction of being recreated in an episode of *The Simpsons*: a bed-ridden Montgomery Burns imitates McDowell while receiving food from his factotum, Smithers.[9] Shortly after McDowell's histrionic eating scene, the film itself becomes distorted as the arrival of the photographers and the gigantic stereo is shot through a fish eye lens [Fig. 18]. The sounds of Beethoven's redemptive music, however, are clear as a bell.

At the end of the twentieth century, *A Clockwork Orange* had achieved cult status, even showing up as a midnight movie in

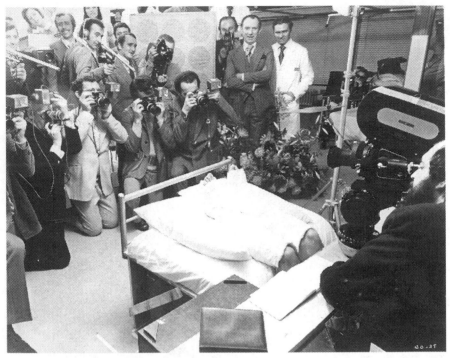

18. Kubrick photographs the photographers.

New York City's Angelica Theatre on the border between Greenwich Village and Soho. But that cult status is probably more related to the film's transgressive, protopunk imagery than to its revisions of the art cinema or its attack on the socialism of pre-Thatcher Britain. Unlike *Paths of Glory* and *Full Metal Jacket*, *A Clockwork Orange* responds not to actual history but to the often solipsistic and contradictory but predominantly aesthetic projects of high modernist art.

NOTES

1   Although Eisenstein was already using rapid progressions of images in the silent era, Louis Malle's *Zazie dans le Métro* (1960) is often credited with inaugurating a passion for rapid montage in the films of the 1960s and 1970s.

2   When Alex is undergoing the early stages of the Ludovico treatment and being made to watch a violent scene from a film, he praises it as "a very good professional piece of sinny like it was done in Hollywood." He then observes, "It's funny how the colors of the real world only seem really real when you viddy them on the screen."

3   Ironically, as of this writing, Malcolm McDowell appears as an archi-
     conservative Harvard English professor on the sitcom *Pearl*, a return vehicle
     for Rhea Perlman, a popular actress in the 1980s sitcoms *Cheers* and *Taxi*.
4   *That's Entertainment!* was released just two years after *A Clockwork Orange*. It
     begins with a celebration of the various versions of "Singin' in the Rain," but
     neither Malcolm McDowell nor Kubrick's film are mentioned. The omission
     is probably related to the fact that *A Clockwork Orange* was released by Warner
     Bros., not by MGM, but the song's prominence was undoubtedly a result of
     its memorable presence in Kubrick's film.
5   The music in *Full Metal Jacket* also includes the memorable marching chants
     of Sgt. Hartman (Lee Ermey), such as "Ho Chi Minh is a son of a bitch/Got
     the blue balls, crabs, and the seven-year itch." The film ends with the soldiers
     walking into battle singing the theme from *The Mickey Mouse Club*.
6   J. Hoberman makes the most convincing case for the unfinished status of
     the film in general and of the music in particular. According to Michael
     Herr, Kubrick called to say that he needed two more weeks before he could
     show the film to Herr: "There was looping to be done and the music wasn't
     finished, lots of small technical fixes on color and sound, but it wasn't ready
     to show" (p. 68). Kubrick died two days after the phone call.
7   Some years after the release of *A Clockwork Orange*, evidence surfaced that
     von Karajan had twice joined the Nazi party. It is extremely unlikely that
     Kubrick was aware of these charges when he filmed *A Clockwork Orange*.
8   Krin Gabbard has explored the relationship between Sellers and Kubrick in
     "The Circulation of Sado-Masochistic Desire in the *Lolita* Texts."
9   Homages to *A Clockwork Orange* have been a regular feature on *The Simpsons*.
     In one episode Bart convinces his father that he should be allowed to stay
     home from school, saying, "Got a pain in me gulliver." In another episode
     Bart's Halloween costume consists of Alex's hat, cane, and false eyelash. And
     in still another, the Ludovico technique, complete with devices to prop open
     the eyes, is used to convert the family's dog, "Santa's Little Helper," into an
     attack dog.

BIBLIOGRAPHY

Baxter, John.1997. *Kubrick: A Biography*. New York: Carroll and Graf, 1997.
Bordwell, David. *Narration and the Fiction Film*. Madison: University of Wisconsin
     Press, 1985.
Burnham, Scott G. *Beethoven Hero*. Princeton: Princeton University Press, 1995.
Gabbard, Krin. "The Circulation of Sado-Masochistic Desire in the *Lolita* Texts."
     Journal of Film and Video 46.2 (1994): 19–30.
Gorbman, Claudia. *Unheard Melodies: Narrative Film Music*. Bloomington: Indiana
     University Press, 1987.
Herr, Michael. *Kubrick*. New York: Grove, 2000.
Hoberman, J. "I Wake Up Dreaming." *Village Voice* July 17, 1999: 117. Available
     at: http://www.villagevoice.com/issues/9929/hoberman.shtml

Joyce, James. *A Portrait of the Artist as a Young Man*. Hammondsworth: Penguin, 1964.

Kael, Pauline. Rev. of *A Clockwork Orange*. *The New Yorker* Jan. 1, 1972: 50–53.

Kalinak, Kathryn. *Settling the Score: Music and the Classical Hollywood Cinema*. Madison: University of Wisconsin Press, 1992.

LoBrutto, Vincent. *Stanley Kubrick: A Biography*. New York: Donald I. Fine, 1997.

Nelson, Thomas Allen. *Kubrick: Inside a Film Artist's Maze*. Bloomington: Indiana University Press, 2000.

North, Anna. Liner notes to *Alex North's 2001: The Legendary Score* (audio CD). Varese Sarabande 5400. 1993.

Ray, Robert B. *A Certain Tendency of the Hollywood Cinema, 1930–1980*. Princeton: Princeton University Press, 1985.

Rosenbaum, Jonathan. Rev. of *Eyes Wide Shut*. *Chicago Reader* July 23, 1999.

Sklar, Robert. "Stanley Kubrick and the American Film Industry." *Current Research in Film* 4 (1988): 114–24.

Strick, Joseph, and Penelope Houston. "Interview with Stanley Kubrick." *Sight and Sound* (Spring 1972): 62–66.

5 "A Bird of Like Rarest Spun Heavenmetal"

Music in A Clockwork Orange

INTRODUCTION: "INVISIBLE REALITIES"

Toward the beginning of Anthony Burgess's A Clockwork Orange, the young protagonist, Alex, describes an ecstatic moment in Geoffrey Plautus's one-movement Violin Concerto: "a bird of like rarest spun heavenmetal, or like silvery wine flowing in a spaceship, gravity all nonsense now, came the violin solo above all the other strings, and those strings were like a cage of silk round my bed" (p. 39; Part 1, Chapter 3). Part of the longest sustained musical passage in the novel, it's a striking account. It's undeniably accurate, too – not because it precisely mirrors the actual score, but rather, paradoxically, because there's no actual score to mirror. For like several other pieces mentioned in the novel – both popular songs and, more important, "classical' works – the Plautus Violin Concerto has no existence in the world outside the novel.

What is the function of such references to imaginary music? Why, for instance, does Burgess use a brief phrase from Das Bettzeug, by the invented composer Friedrich Gitterfenster, to trigger the crucial fight between Alex and Dim (p. 33; Part 1, Chapter 3)? One might plausibly think that such allusions serve primarily to reinforce the futuristic aura of Burgess's invented "nadsat" language. As Burgess was acutely aware, any slang, no matter how trendy at the time a novel is written, can quickly become stale and appear outdated. Thus, in order to sustain the illusion that the novel takes place in some indefinite future, even for readers reading decades after its composition, Burgess devised "an appropriate idiolect" that could not be tied in the reader's mind to any historical milieu (*Clockwork: A Play*, p. v).[1] Reference to actual works of music as contemporary, of course, would suffer in the same way from rapid obsolescence. Burgess's decision to throw in allusions to the Claudius Birdman String Quartet (p. 48; Part 1, Chapter 4) or Ike Yard's "Honey Nose" (p. 52; Part 1, Chapter 4), rather than to a new piece by Milhaud or a new song by Elvis Presley, neatly solves the problem by divorcing his novel from any historically specifiable musical environment.[2]

That's undoubtedly one explanation for the presence of the imaginary music. There's a more important rhetorical reason for this practice, however: it helps moderate our antipathy to Alex's violence and thus helps support the fundamental ambiguity on which the novel's complex moral effects depend. For brief as it is, the description of the Plautus Concerto opens up a bittersweet glimpse of a nonexistent world we cannot have, the kind of vision described by Vladimir Nabokov, in "Cloud, Castle, Lake," a short story about totalitarian destruction of such visions, as a happiness "once half dreamt" (p. 87). Such visions of "rarest spun heavenmetal" do more than merely provide Alex with the "deep and poetical sensitivity to music" that Jackson Burgess (no relation) saw as "the only gesture toward 'significance'" in the film version (p. 33). That is, the ability to appreciate the Plautus Concerto is not just one more character trait that Alex possesses. It is, rather, a rhetorical position he inhabits in the narrative, one that makes the readers depend on him – for the audience wishes, at least with regard to this aspect of Alex's life, to be where he is and to hear what he hears. Alex is our sole guide into the music of Geoffrey Plautus; his closeness to the happiness "once half dreamt," coupled with our need to experience it through him if we are to experience it at all, nourishes in the reader a certain envy, even admiration and sympathy.

This dependence is then used to manipulate the audience as the novel works through issues of free will. Specifically, this dependence creates one important counterbalance to the antipathy Burgess wants his readers to feel toward Alex's acts of violence, and thus serves – along with, for instance, Alex's poetic language and the unsympathetic portrayal of both competing political camps in the novel – as one more pivot on which the philosophical and political ambiguity of the novel rests.

What happens when a novel studded with such rarified imaginary music is filmed? Soundtracks require actual music; so the formal shift from narrative to cinema necessarily eliminates the possibility of treating imaginary music *as* imaginary music. What choices does a filmmaker then have?[3] There are, I believe, two basic alternatives. The first is to make the imaginary music real by *composing* equivalents for the nonexistent scores. But as Volker Schloendorff's film version of Marcel Proust's *Swann in Love* (1984) makes clear, this is a risky course, even with the cooperation of a composer of Hans Werner Henze's stature. Proust's evocations of the music of Vinteuil, in particular the "little phrase" in the Violin Sonata, are similar to Alex's evocations of Plautus and Gitterfenster – in fact, they may well have served as Burgess's model. When Swann encounters the Sonata unexpectedly at the Marquise de Saint-Euverte's party, for instance, Proust describes the moment as follows:

> Suddenly it was as though she [Odette] had entered, and this apparition was so agonizingly painful that his hand clutched at his heart. The violin had risen to a series of high notes on which it rested as though awaiting something, holding on to them in a prolonged expectancy, in the exaltation of already seeing the object of its expectation approaching, and with a desperate effort to last out until its arrival, to welcome it before itself expiring, to keep the way open for a moment longer.[4]
>
> (p. 490)

And the failure of Henze's impersonation of Vinteuil reminds us that music of such subtle rapture cannot be created on commission: it is not possible to demand a new work that can make a listener feel as Swann feels when he hears this phrase, "the presence of one of those invisible realities in which he had ceased to believe" (Proust, p. 298). Much less is it possible to reproduce our complex reliance on the character involved as our guide to the music, for once it is actualized, we are free to hear it for ourselves.

It was thus eminently reasonable for Kubrick to take the second path: elimination of the imaginary music. Yes, there are brief allusions, both visual and verbal, to nonexistent pop performers in

19. Alex prepares to ask Marty and Sonietta home with him for a little fun and music.

the record-store scene [Fig. 19]; but Kubrick erases the references to Plautus, Gitterfenster, and their invented classical-music colleagues and substitutes a certified Great Work (Beethoven's Ninth) in the three major scenes where some kind of music was necessary: the scene where Alex lashes out at Dim in the Korova Milkbar, the "heavenmetal" masturbation scene that follows his evening rampage, and the torture scene that leads to his attempted suicide.

It is a sign of Kubrick's skill as an adapter that he was able to find alternative, medium-specific mechanisms to compensate for what he had to abandon. Creating the futuristic effect was fairly straightforward: he commissioned Walter (Wendy) Carlos to craft eerie electronic versions of classical masterpieces, the most striking of which is probably the adaptation of Purcell (*Music for the Funeral of Queen Mary*) that launches the film and returns, in a variety of guises, as a leitmotif throughout.[5] Compensating for rhetorical balance, however, was more complex, and the results are more interesting. In the film, the moments "once half dreamt" no longer exist – and as a consequence, that poignant sense of an invisible (or inaudible) distant reality, and the audience's sympathetic desire to be in Alex's position,

are erased. This ebb in sympathy for Alex is magnified by the film's reduced reliance on Alex's poetic but often opaque style. The language
itself, after all, serves to mask his violence in unfamiliar words: as
Burgess himself put it, "to *tolchock* a *chelloveck* in the *kishkas* does not
sound so bad as booting a man in the guts, and the *old in-out in-out*,
even if it reduces the sexual act to a mechanical action, does not
sicken quite so much as a Harold Robbins description of cold rape"
(*Clockwork: A Play*, pp. viii–ix). The fact that the violence in the film
is visual, and hence more immediate, only puts further pressure on
Kubrick to find some way of rebalancing our relation to Alex.

One technique was to play up the charm and charisma of actor
Malcolm McDowell. Even in his profoundly negative review, Robert
Hatch praised him as "loathsomely attractive" (p. 28). But Kubrick
also relied, albeit in a different way from Burgess, on music as a means
of countering our antipathy to Alex's violence. As Don Heckman puts
it, Kubrick

> has an unusually vivid awareness of the effectiveness of background
> music. Over and over again, ... he has employed fragments of clas-
> sical music, pop songs, straight background scoring, sound effects,
> electronics and the like not only for atmosphere, but to act as emo-
> tional counterpoint to the happenings that are taking place on the
> screen.
>
> (p. 20)

Specifically, since he was limited to audible music, Kubrick took
advantage of its manipulative potential, wrapping the violence in
familiar scores that could serve to distance us from it. As Robert P.
Kolker puts it in his essay elsewhere in this volume, the "civility" of
the music is "used to surround the brutality of the modern world"
(p. 30). Thus, the fight with Billy Boy and his droogs and the following night ride are "emotionally counterpointed," to borrow
Heckman's phrase, against the overture to *La gazza ladra* (*The Thieving
Magpie*), by the nineteenth-century Italian composer Rossini; so are
the fight with his own gang and the murder. And the orgy-turned-
rape with the two young girls he picks up at the record store has its
emotional counterpoint in Rossini's *William Tell* Overture.

There is little doubt that these two compensatory techniques –
Kubrick's canny use of Carlos's score and his deployment of standards

from the classical repertoire – do help offset for the loss of the imaginary music. But like any adaptation or rewriting of a work of art, they do so at a cost. For in addition to conjuring up images of a future and supporting our ambivalence toward Alex, Burgess's use of imaginary music has a third, less immediately obvious function in the novel as well, a contribution to the novel's aesthetic argument. And it's this argument that I address in some detail for the remainder of this essay.

To understand what is at stake here, we must first recognize an important, but often overlooked, strand of the novel's content. *A Clockwork Orange* is "about" many things. Burgess himself dubbed it "a sort of allegory of Christian free will" (*Clockwork: A Play*, p. vii); it's also a study of urban social decay, an examination of what Margaret DeRosia calls the "erotics of violence" (p. 61), and a commentary on a particular prepunk moment in British political and cultural history, when "the hooligan groups known as the Teddyboys and the Mods and Rockers" (*Clockwork: A Play*, p. v) represented adolescent extremes.[6] But this early novel, which Burgess, a skilled composer himself, ruefully compared to the Rachmaninoff Prelude in C-sharp Minor (a similarly youthful success that the mature Rachmaninoff could never live down) (*Clockwork*, p. v),[7] is also very profoundly a book about music. Specifically, Burgess's novel – arguably written in sonata form[8] – is an exploration of certain violent undercurrents in the German musical tradition, an exploration tied to certain philosophical claims about the act of listening.

As I show, the imaginary music serves as a key element in Burgess's attempt to articulate his aesthetic position. And while Kubrick manages to compensate for the first two functions of imaginary music, he ends up neglecting the third. Indeed, he does more than neglect it: his compensatory techniques in the film distort, even invert, the aesthetic arguments that Burgess is presenting in the novel. In part, as I argue, that is because Kubrick's film eliminates the final chapter; in part, it's because Kubrick isn't really "keen on music" in the way Alex is (*Clockwork*, p. 131, Part 2, Chapter 6), and in his choice of repertoire, he disregards musical distinctions that are central to Burgess's argument. But more interesting, the distortion stems as well from the shift in medium from novel to film. Let me stress that the point of my argument is not to take Kubrick to task for lack of accuracy: fidelity in cinematic adaptations is not necessarily a virtue. Nonetheless, the

choices Kubrick has made, however we judge them, do have intellectual consequences, and it is surely worthwhile asking ourselves what
they are.

THEORETICAL DETOUR: RAVEL'S BIRDS

In order to explain Burgess's position and Kubrick's distortion, however, I need to take a brief theoretical detour to explain the process
of listening to music. In the framework that Jay Reise and I have developed (see, for instance, "Phonograph"), there are three primary
components to musical experience. First, any work of music exists
as a concrete entity, with what we call *technical* attributes – those
characteristics of the sound (for instance, pitch, rhythm, and timbre)
that can be captured in written notation. It is the technical level that
makes the music audible. But the audible is not necessarily compre-
hensible. The technical is, in fact, meaningless raw material, without
shape or consequence, until it is processed by the listener through
the application of shared, culturally determined interpretive conventions that assign meanings to the actual sounds. We call this second
component the *attributive* level. Thus, to take a simple example, an
elementary set of notes played on a bugle, when heard through the
appropriate interpretive conventions, comes to be "heard as" "Taps"
and hence to "mean" closure.

Reise and I use the word "meaning" in a fairly wide sense: the attributive informs listening even when we are not dealing with such
referential meanings as those evoked by "Taps." In fact, attributive
processes intervene in our listening even on the level of harmony.
A G Major chord heard in a C Major piece has a certain technical
sound; but its "meaning" – in particular, the pressure which pushes
it to resolve to C – is something that's learned through experience in
a culture. Reise and I call this kind of attributive information *codes*,
the "regulations" of conventional behavior that can be determined
through statistical analysis. Thus, near the beginning of his familiar
harmony textbook, Walter Piston serves up a chart so that fledgling
composers will know the relative intensity with which they can as-
sume listeners will expect certain progressions. But it's not based
on anything essential in the music itself; rather, it's derived from
"observations of usage" – that is, it is based on the relative frequency

of particular progressions in Western tonal music of the eighteenth and nineteenth centuries (Piston, p. 18). More relevant to my argument here, however, is a second type of attributive information – and we realize that the distinction is a loose one – that Reise and I call the "mythological." The mythological consists of the discourse that surrounds the music we hear, the cultural apparatus that serves as part of the framework within which we understand and interpret it: the historical "fact" that Benjamin Britten wrote many of his most important tenor parts for his lover, Peter Pears, the stories about Elvis Presley's addictions, the influential Disney-fabricated Mickey Mouse images that many listeners associate with Dukas's *Sorcerer's Apprentice*, or the influential Kubrick-fabricated images that many listeners associate with Richard Strauss's *Also Sprach Zarathustra*.

Listening, however, is an active interpretive process; although it always involves the technical and the attributive layers, the existence of those two components only provides the possibility for music. It is the listener who actualizes that potential, who applies particular attributive screens to the particular sounds at hand in order to come up with a particular experience. Reise and I call this third aspect the *synthetic* component of listening.

Synthetic acts differ from one another in many ways, but three synthetic dimensions are especially important for an understanding of the aesthetic arguments in *A Clockwork Orange*. First, listeners can differ with regard to the relative importance of the technical and attributive. For instance, if you ask a group of people what they hear when they hear the rhythm of the first movement of Gustav Holst's *The Planets*, one might simply reproduce the technical by tapping it out; another might explain the music in terms of codes, describing its repeated metrical structure; a third, especially if he or she listens through the title ("Mars"), might hear the rhythms simply as "militaristic." In fact, as I've discovered, many listeners hear this music so mythologically that they are unable to reproduce the technical at all or even to recognize that the piece is in quintuple meter.[9]

Second, synthetic acts of listening differ with respect to how self-consciously the listener applies attributive information. Two listeners hearing the daybreak music of Maurice Ravel's *Daphnis and Chloë*, for instance, may both hear birdcalls in the musical texture, but one might believe the reference to be largely technical (that is, he or she might hear the sounds as a more-or-less direct mimicry of the sounds of actual birds), while the other might recognize that Ravel is calling upon stock gestures that are culturally associated with birds.

Finally, of course, listeners can differ with regard to the particular attributive strands they choose to apply. The listener who hears the opening of *Also Sprach Zarathustra* through Strauss's précis of Nietzsche, for instance, will have a significantly different experience than the listener who hears it through Kubrick's imagery.

Although listeners ultimately steer their own synthetic courses, different composers invite different synthetic strategies in all three of these dimensions. By titling his symphonic triptych *La Mer* (*The Sea*), for instance, Debussy was inviting us to hear his music, strongly and self-consciously, through particular visual images. By calling his Fifth Symphony a "symphony," Beethoven was also inviting us to apply particular interpretive strategies, although the screens called up by the word "symphony" – for instance, the implicit invitation to map out the first movement's sounds according to the patterns of sonata form – are less mythological and less self-consciously attributive than those called up by the words "the sea." The aggressively nondescriptive titles of much avant-garde music of the 1950s – for instance, Milton Babbitt's *Composition for Four Instruments* – seem quixotically aimed at discouraging the use of any attributive screens whatever.

But it is not only composers who invite particular synthetic strategies. Different theorists of music encourage us to synthesize in different ways as well. Thus, one can read nineteenth-century debates about what, if anything, music depicts – for instance, Eduard Hanslick's insistence that music could be compared to a kaleidoscope, since it "consists wholly of sounds artistically combined" (p. 47) without representing anything outside itself – as debates about how significant and self-conscious the attributive layer ought to be.

PARADOX AND RESOLUTION: "VERY QUIET AND LIKE YEARNY"

Indeed, music criticism more generally can be viewed as a series of disputes over appropriate attributive screens, disputes in which Burgess's novel vigorously participates. Specifically, *A Clockwork Orange* proposes certain synthetic activities in order to provide a sobering meditation on the relationship between violence and the particular musical tradition to which Alex is most attached – the Austro-German symphonic tradition sketched out by the flunky who brings Alex the stereo after his cure: "'What shall it be? . . . Mozart? Beethoven? Schoenberg? Carl Orff?'" (p. 204; Part 3, Chapter 6). For although Alex does not realize it when he undergoes the Ludovico treatment, the use of Beethoven – a linchpin of that tradition – as a background for Nazi films is not simply a coincidence. German music and German atrocities cannot be easily disassociated.[10]

Burgess's general analysis of the connection between violence and German music is closely tied to certain specific synthetic activities that Alex performs – and the rhetorical power of those synthetic acts is, in turn, tied to his use of imaginary music, which significantly colors the way we are encouraged to think about listening. How does this happen? Normally, a verbal description of a work of music – even one that comes from the composer – provides only one possible attributive screen, one way of hearing the technical. In the case of imaginary music like the Vinteuil Sonata or the Plautus Violin Concerto, however, it provides the *only* way of "hearing" it. That is, since the imaginary works have no technical layer, reference to them tilts the balance of listening strongly and self-consciously to the mythological level. As we try, as readers, to imagine listening to the Plautus Violin Concerto, there is no way for us to imagine that we are listening simply to a kaleidoscope of "sounds artistically combined," since, as happens in Proust, the imagined listening experience transcends corporeal notes entirely. We are forced to recognize the attributive aspects of Alex's experience – and consequently of our own listening as well.

At the same time, as I have already pointed out, the imaginary music creates a sense of dependence on our guide. As happens in other novels where a narrator takes us places to which we have no easy alternative access – for instance, when Marlow leads us up the river in Joseph Conrad's *Heart of Darkness* – we are forced to accept his or her assessments, even when we have plenty of reason to doubt his or her reliability. Since we are forced to accept Alex's attributive screens for Plautus, we are apt, through the pressure of inertia, to do so elsewhere in the novel as well, even when Alex is writing about music that actually *does* exist in the world outside the novel. That's especially likely to happen in the novel (as opposed to the film), since even with real music, the technical strand isn't immediately "there" on the page to contradict any attributive claims made about it. And given our musical dependence on Alex earlier, few readers are likely to conjure up the actual sounds of Bach's *Brandenburg* "just for middle and lower strings" (the *Sixth*) to decide whether to accept Alex's attributive description that it is "starry and strong and very firm" (p. 40; Part 1, Chapter 3).

What particular screens does Alex provide? Actually, he offers us two different kinds of attributive screens. First, we have what might be called, for lack of a better term, a cultural-historical screen. Certainly, the decision to separate out German classical music as a category is a synthetic act – one that encourages us to listen to music in terms of musical history, national borders, and a series of charged hierarchies, including the distinction between popular and classical music. And that screen has a significant impact on the way Alex thinks about music.

Second, and more provocative, Alex offers a set of what might be called "ethical" attributions, using the term ethical in the broad sense, which, as Wayne C. Booth aptly puts it, refers not simply to morals or to "the approved side of choices," but rather to "the entire range of effects on the 'character' or 'person' or 'self'" (p. 8). In fact, Alex offers us a pair of competing ethical screens. On the one hand, we have the "crashing and howling" (p. 54; Part 1, Chapter 4) attributive screen, a way of listening to music as a spur to violence that is always near to hand. Listening to Mozart's *Jupiter* Symphony, he sees "new pictures of different litsos to be ground and splashed" (p. 40; Part 1, Chapter 3); listening to the Sixth Brandenburg, he realizes that he should have been fiercer in his attack earlier in the evening: "I would like to have tolchocked them both harder and ripped them to ribbons on their own floor" (p. 40; Part 1, Chapter 3).

At first, these violent responses might appear to be purely idiosyncratic. Why, for instance, should hearing a bar of the Beethoven Violin Concerto from a passing car inspire Alex to pull out his razor and attack Georgie (p. 61; Part 1, Chapter 5)? But in fact, Burgess's novel fits into a long and substantial philosophical tradition, going back at least to Plato's attack on music in *The Republic*, of considering the emotional and ethical dangers of music. *A Clockwork Orange* participates more directly in a shorter, more specific, critical tradition that probes the tie between the classical German tradition and masculine violence. That narrower tradition is vividly represented by Tolstoy's *Kreutzer Sonata*, a short novel in which Beethoven's "terrible" music serves as a catalyst for murder by opening up "new feelings, new possibilities" in the narrator (p. 219–220; Chapter 23). Similar issues are raised in James M. Cain's *Serenade*, with its shocking image of beauty, including specifically Beethoven's music, as a shark "that carries death with every move that it makes" (p. 79; Chapter 6). More abstractly, this tradition continues among feminist musicologists today. Susan McClary, for instance, has argued that such nineteenth-century composers as Beethoven (especially in the Ninth) "quite regularly push mechanisms of frustration to the limit, such that desire in their narratives frequently culminates (as though necessarily) in explosive violence" (p. 127). In Burgess's novel, Alex's accidental discovery that Beethoven and Nazi propaganda films are closely intertwined similarly reveals that broader cultural forces are at play here.

At the same time, though, as I have suggested in my discussion of imaginary music, Burgess offers us brief glimpses of a second, alternative ethical screen. This screen is found, for instance, in the early part of the description of the Plautus Concerto, before Alex falls back into his more violent listening habits: an ethereal, poetic way of listening to music as an exquisite, harmonic otherworld, "a bird of like rarest spun heavenmetal," always just beyond our reach. It's this alternative way of listening that redeems music as a cultural practice, and Alex's spiritual journey, to a certain extent, is a journey toward resolution of the tension between these two apparently contradictory screens and a recognition of the primacy of the second. Geoffrey Plautus is described as an American composer, which might at first seem to suggest that this second ethical screen is best found in non-German music. That may be true; but the novel indicates that Alex eventually learns to find his peace with German music as well. For the final chapter shows a transformed Alex, less intent on listening to music for large orchestra, "lying on the bed between the violins and the trombones and kettledrums" (p. 213; Part 3, Chapter 7). Instead, he finds himself "slooshying more like malenky romantic songs, what they call *Lieder*, just a goloss and a piano, very quiet and like yearny" (212–213; Part 3, Chapter 7). As Burgess himself puts it, borrowing the Apollonian/Dionysian distinction that Nietzsche employed in *The Birth of Tragedy*, "Alex's aggressive instincts have been stimulated by classical music, but the music has been forewarning him of what he must some day become: a man who recognizes the Dionysiac in, say, Beethoven but appreciates the Apollonian as well" (*Clockwork: A Play*, p. x).

It's in the special interaction between these two ethical screens that Burgess's twist on conventional musical thinking can be seen. He does not, at least in this novel, share Cain's macho love of the danger lurking under the music; nor does he share Tolstoy's and McClary's censure of the violent elements in German music; nor, for that matter, does he believe that the highest art, like tragedy and Wagnerian opera for Nietzsche, offers a complex synthesis of the wild, intoxicating Dionysian and the more serene Apollonian.[11] Rather, Burgess's point is that just as free moral choice requires the possibility of choosing evil, so the attainment of the highest artistic achievement, at least within the terms of the German musical canon, depends on the simultaneous possibility of unleashing destructive forces. As Enderby puts it in *The Clockwork Testament*, one has the choice to "die with Beethoven's Ninth howling and crashing away or live in a safe world of silly clockwork music" (*Testament*, p. 117, Chapter 8). Or, to put it in *Star Wars* terms: the power of the Force for good depends, in a fundamental way, on the existence of the dark side. The crashing and howling may be problematic, but without it, there's no possibility of heavenmetal.[12]

My purpose here is not to explicate in detail the process by which Alex comes to this reconciliation. Nor is it to evaluate the validity of Burgess's arguments or the quality of the crucial last chapter, which many critics have found unconvincing. Rather, my point is that, however one feels about it, Alex's turn to music that's "quiet and like yearny" lies at the heart of the musical argument in the novel, and that Kubrick's film offers us a musical perspective that is altogether different.

THE KUBRICK ALTERNATIVE: "EMOTIONAL COUNTERPOINT"

The film alters the novel's trajectory in three ways. First, and most obviously, Kubrick ignores the last chapter, leaving Alex as an unreconstructed Dionysiac poised for a return to a life of violence. Kubrick didn't even find out about the textual crux until he had nearly finished the screenplay, and he retroactively decided that it couldn't

have been important anyway. Branding the last chapter "unconvincing and inconsistent with the style and intent of the book," he went
on to suggest (in a reversal of Burgess's own account) that Burgess
himself was not committed to it: "I wouldn't be surprised to learn that
the publisher had somehow prevailed upon Burgess to tack on the
extra chapter against his better judgment, so the book would end on
a more positive note. I certainly never gave any serious consideration
to using it" (Ciment, p. 157).

Second, even if the last chapter *had* been included in the film,
Burgess's argument would not have been reproduced, because
Kubrick's choice of repertoire betrays an insensitivity to the musical
categories so important to Alex and his creator. At first, it might seem
strange to accuse Kubrick of musical insensitivity. After all, many
of his films are justly celebrated for their integration of music and
image – so much so that many listeners identify the opening of *Also
Sprach Zarathustra* with Kubrick's film *2001* rather than with its composer, Richard Strauss. And the film of *Clockwork Orange* is full of
jokes for the musically minded: for instance, the doorbell in the
home where Alex and his droogs assault the author and his wife
rings out the opening motif of Beethoven's Fifth. Yet while Kubrick
loves to filch what he calls "the great orchestral music of the past
and present" (Ciment, p. 153) for his soundtracks (in this regard,
his choice of Rossini's *Thieving Magpie* is richly appropriate), his relationship to music is quite different from Burgess's. And although
the film does make considerable use of "the glorious Ninth" (p. 204;
Part 3, Chapter 6), one of Alex's touchstones, Kubrick's soundtrack for
this film reflects a musical taste that's incompatible with the novel's,
mapping out the world of music according to a far different historical-
cultural attributive screen.

Specifically, the film works with broader musical categories and
hence offers a less precise sense of the shape of the classical canon.
This may be due, in part, to Kubrick's belief that German music
can, in fact, be separated out from the history of German culture.[13]
When Michel Ciment observed that Kubrick's films "seem to show
an attraction for Germany: the German music, the characters of
Dr. Strangelove, Professor Zempf in *Lolita*," Kubrick responded that,
while not "attracted," he did "share the fairly widespread fascination
with the horror of the Nazi period." But he detached German music from the National Socialist nexus: "I wouldn't include German

music as a relevant part of that group" (Ciment, p. 156). While he recognizes a paradox between Nazi atrocities and Nazi high culture, he apparently believes the contradiction to lie in the general "failure of culture to have any morally refining effect on society. Hitler loved good music and many top Nazis were cultured and sophisticated men but it didn't do them, or anyone else, much good" (Ciments, p. 163). In other words, for Kubrick the *specific* works of "good" music they loved – the Beethoven, Bruckner, and Wagner – are a random and irrelevant historical accident. Beethoven, in Kubrick's film, stands in for "good music" in the most general sense; he is not a central figure, as he appears to be for Burgess, in a *national* tradition that often defined itself in opposition to the music, say, from France or Rossini's Italy.

Whether or not this attitude toward German music influenced the choice of music for the film, it is undeniable that the film's eclectic array of music blurs the lines separating the cultural-historical categories so important to Burgess. Donald Costello argues that in the film, music "is stripped of human resonance – any type of music fitting any mood: Elgar in a prison corridor, 'Singin' in the Rain' during rape and beating, Beethoven during the cutting of friends" (p. 385). Given the way that *The Thieving Magpie* and *William Tell* are, as we've seen, deployed as a way to defuse the filmic violence (in fact, in the film it is Rossini, not Beethoven, who provides the backdrop to the slow motion "cutting of friends"), it's hard to agree that the soundtrack is quite that random. But there is little doubt that Kubrick's extensive use of Rossini (a composer for whom the Germanophilic Alex would probably have only contempt) provides a substantively different mapping of musical terrain from the one we find in the original novel.

So, even more so, does the film's famous incorporation of "Singin' in the Rain." Many critics (e.g., Nelson, p. 151ff) have argued that the film presents Alex as a performer. Mario Falsetto suggests, more specifically, that "he views himself perhaps as a rock star or performance artist" (p. 153). That's an astute observation about the film, but it's a far cry from the Alex of the novel, who is very much a *consumer* of music, and who in any case has the greatest contempt for rock and pop, which, from his perspective, barely deserve the designation "music" (p. 7, Part 1, Chapter 1). There's an almost visceral sense of disgust, for instance, when Alex finds himself playing

Marty's and Sonietta's "pathetic" pop discs on his high-end stereo: it's "like peeting some sweet scented kid's drink . . . in like very beautiful and lovely and costly gold goblets" (p. 52, Part 1, Chapter 4).[14] The choice of "Singin' in the Rain" during the rape scene certainly does not reflect the character Alex's elite musical sensitivity; rather – and this is a revealing bit of cinematic trivia – it reflects the actor Malcolm McDowell's lack thereof. As McDowell described the decision to include it:

> When we got to the scene where the writer is beaten and his wife raped, Stanley suddenly called, "Hey, Malcolm, can you sing and dance?" I can't do either. I said, "Oh, yes, Stanley, sure," and just sort of started dancing, then kicking the writer. And I began "Singin' in the Rain," as it's the only song I know. Within three hours, Stanley had bought the rights to it. (Burke, p. 13).

When the tastes of an actor, who knows only a single song, takes the place of a character for whom music is central, it's no wonder that the musical argument is skewed.

Over and above the elimination of the final chapter and the remapping of musical categories to mush the distinctions between German and Italian, classical and popular, there is a third, and more interesting if more complicated, way in which the film alters the musicality of the novel: in part because of the shift in medium, it shifts the novel's arguments by encouraging very different synthetic activities on the ethical plane.

As I've said, Burgess's novel, in part through its deployment of imaginary music, stresses self-conscious mythological listening and offers a pair of complementary ethical attributive screens to explain both the danger and the value of German music. Because it has to eliminate the imaginary music, the film changes the way we are encouraged to listen by tilting the balance back from the attributive and especially from our self-conscious awareness of the mythological. It's not simply that we hear the music; furthermore, as on most soundtracks, we are discouraged from thinking about it directly, since most of the time – especially in the three Rossini-cushioned scenes – the music is background, rather than foreground, material.[15] There are perhaps two exceptions. Parts of the novel's descriptions of Plautus and Gitterfenster are applied to the Ninth in two scenes in the film where Beethoven takes over for the imaginary composers. But for the most part, the ethical screens through which we are encouraged to process the soundtrack are those that most automatically come to mind. Instead of providing new and intellectually challenging ethical screens, as the novel does, the film makes us take old attributive screens for granted, as if they were part of the technical.

For instance, I mentioned earlier that Kubrick uses music to neutralize the violence – and it's worth paying attention to how he does so. As Kubrick himself puts it, in a discussion of the attempted rape and the fight with Billy Boy and his droogs, the violence is "stylized" through the music, which serves as a substitute for Burgess's "writing style": "You could say that the violence is turned into dance" (Houston, p. 43).[16] As Kolker puts it, the fight is a "staged, balletic performance" (ms. p. 32). In this regard, it's not insignificant that, as Bernard Beck points out, the attempted gang rape takes place "on a literal stage to a background of *theatrical* music" (p. 41, italics added). Similarly, when he was asked why he filmed the "orgy" scene in high speed, Kubrick noted that "It seemed to me a good way to satirize what had become the fairly common use of slow-motion to solemnize this sort of thing, and turn it into 'art.' The *William Tell* Overture also seemed a good musical joke to counter the standard Bach accompaniment" (Ciment, pp. 151–152).

Leaving aside the question of what films have promoted Bach as the "standard ... accompaniment" for such scenes, the basic rhetorical principle here is clear: the music is a "joke" that serves to soften the violence. And how does the music become a joke? Through the ethical attributive associations with which it is already loaded, even before we start to watch the film, and which make a satirical emotional counterpoint to the visual elements. In other words, as in the gang fight, we are asked to take Rossini's light-hearted inappropriateness as a given, as a technical element, and not to recognize the degree to which that light-heartedness is socially constructed. (In this regard, it's worth noting that neither *The Thieving Magpie* nor *William Tell* are comic operas, although the overtures have come to be received into our culture as lightweight affairs). Similarly, in Kubrick's film we're asked to take Beethoven's high moral purpose for granted and to see the juxtaposition of Beethoven's *Ninth* and Alex's images of sex and violence as an ironic counterpoint, not – as in Tolstoy, Cain, McClary, and Burgess – as a trace of something dark and dangerous lurking within Beethoven and the German classical tradition.[17]

Much the same process of *assuming*, rather than creating, ethical attributive screens can be seen in the use of Elgar in the prison and hospital scenes: the music has been chosen primarily because it could be expected to call up stock associations of pomp for the viewer. And the same thing happens in the Biblical epics that Alex imagines. Here the soundtrack gives us snippets from Rimsky-Korsakov's *Sheherezade*. Thomas Allen Nelson justifies the juxtaposition on the grounds that "Rimsky-Korsakov is the Miklos Rozsa of classical music" (p. 156). Whether this condescending observation is fair to Rimsky-Korsakov (or to Rozsa, the distinguished composer of numerous concert works as well as the classic scores to such films as *Ben Hur* and *Lost Weekend*), or whether Burgess's Alex would ever fantasize to such music, Nelson's observation is on target with regard to the broad culture. That is, he is right about the attributive screens that the audience is likely already to have before they come into the theater. And the intended ironies of Kubrick's film – the emotional counterpoint between sound and image, the stylization that moderates the impact of the violence – leans on those attributions rather than challenges them. The viewer is never asked to interrogate Beethoven, but only to accept his status as a cultural icon of Great Art and high moral worth. And while it's hard to know for sure whether actual viewers have in fact listened as the film encourages them to do, it does seem that most critics who have written about the film – for instance, Charles Austin, who refers to "classical themes so inappropriate that they are perfect" (p. 207) – have accepted these automatic screens without question.

To put it in different terms: for Kubrick the music is a means, not an end. That is, if Burgess's philosophical intent is to use the violence to raise serious questions about music, Kubrick's film does just the opposite: it uses prepackaged associations with music to manipulate the viewer's relation to the violence. In a significant way, then, the film actually reverses the argument of the book, for it uncritically participates in precisely that cultural phenomenon – the one seen, at its worst, in the use of Beethoven to give cultural credibility to Nazi propaganda films – that the novel is holding up for our scrutiny.

For Burgess, Beethoven's greatness (and the greatness of the German musical tradition more generally) is a hard-won quality that is forged out of danger. For Kubrick, Beethoven's greatness is a cultural given that can be used to stave off danger. Under the circumstances, despite the film's undeniable brilliance, one can appreciate Burgess's antipathy to it and understand why he called it a "misdemeanour" (Burgess, *Clockwork*, p. vii). More precisely, we can understand why, in Burgess's own 1986 dramatic adaptation of the novel, Kubrick appears at the very end, performing "in exquisite counterpoint, "Singin' in the Rain" on a trumpet" – only to be "kicked off the stage" (p. 48).

ACKNOWLEDGMENTS

Thanks to Anne Marcoline and Kara Stanek for their research assistance; thanks, too, to Elizabeth Jensen, Maureen Miller, Nancy Sorkin Rabinowitz, Jay Reise, Ernest Williams, and especially Michael Rabinowitz for their help in sharpening the argument.

NOTES

1 His technique was an undeniable success, for the language seems less out of date than that, say, in Irving Welsh's *Trainspotting*, written more than thirty years later.
2 See, with regard to music's transience, Nelson's critique of Kubrick's early film *Killer's Kiss*: "the use of fifties 'jive' music, punctuated by loud blasts from a saxophone, has a low-budget desperation about it and severely dates the film" (p. 29).
3 If, in the analysis that follows, I tend to ignore Burgess's own attempts to provide a dramatic equivalent of his novel, it is for two reasons. First, the plays were written thirty years or so after the novel – by an author whose novelistic experience and public success (with this work in particular) had changed the way he viewed his youthful effort. Second, the author himself seems to have had little faith in the rewrites. He admitted to "a certain gloom about visual adaptation of my little book" – and initially decided to dramatize it only "to stem the flow of amateur adaptations that I have heard about though never seen" (*Clockwork: A Play*, p. ix). For a fuller discussion of the variants, see Hutchings.
4 The similarity between Proust and Burgess is especially obvious when we compare the first sentence here to Alex's description of the phrase from *Das Bettzeug*: "It was like for a moment...some great bird had flown into the milkbar, and I felt all the little malenky hairs on my plott standing endwise

and the shivers crawling up like slow malenky lizards and then down again" (p. 33; Part 1, Chapter 3).

5 This was a gamble, since in retrospect Carlos's adaptations have a distinctly early 1970s feel. They still work because they are conventionally "futuristic" in sound – but it is hard to know how long they will do so. It's always easier, of course, to create an air of the old-fashioned than an aura of the future: The self-consciously creaky "I Want to Marry a Lighthouse Keeper," by Erika Eigen (a pseudonym?), is therefore a more dependable marker, since its function is to underscore the outdated tastes of Alex's parents and Joe.

6 See Nehring's claim that Burgess's memory here is faulty, since the Mods and Rockers "only appeared in the popular press two years after he published the novel" (p. 93).

7 He drew the same parallel between his novel and Beethoven's Minuet in G, although the minuet never quite had the inescapable presence in Beethoven's life that the Prelude in C-sharp Minor and *Clockwork Orange* had in Rachmaninoff's and Burgess's.

8 Many critics talk about the general symmetry of the novel, and of the film as well. Falsetto points out that "the film is, in some ways, structured around actions and their reversals. Several sequences in part one . . . are repeated with variations in part three" (p. 21). Likewise, Ciment points out that Kubrick has a "fascination with symmetry" and refers to *A Clockwork Orange* as "a model of balance – three sections lasting forty-five minutes each, with the central panel of the triptych (the prison and the cure) separating two trajectories each of whose elements is matched in the other if in a different order" (p. 97). In their essay elsewhere in this volume, Krin Gabbard and Shailja Sharma claim that the "symmetrical progression" is so strong that it "violates the narrative credibility of conventional Realist fiction" (ms. p. 87). Vincent Canby makes the claim in more musical terms: the film is "as formally structured" as Beethoven (p. 44). In fact, as is announced by the fact that each section of the novel begins with the same thematic statement ("'What's it going to be then, eh?'"), the three parts of the novel can be seen, more specifically, to mirror the exposition/development/recapitulation pattern of trational sonata form, with the twenty-first chapter as a coda. This is not the place for a detailed analysis, but in general the outer sections employ the same events in much the same order, the central section modulates further afield, although without abandoning the novel's thematic core. See also Burgess's imitation of Beethoven in *Napoleon* Symphony.

9 Meter might appear to be a technical phenomenon, but dividing a musical event into substructures based on rhythmic repetitions is an interpretive act and hence an example of listening through codes.

10 Burgess, later on, *did* attempt to make a clearer disassociation by distinguishing between two types of goodness, aesthetic and moral. As Enderby puts it in *The Clockwork Testament*, "'Well, there are some stupid bastards who can't understand how the commandant of a Nazi concentration camp could go home after torturing Jews all day and then weep tears of joy at a Schubert symphony on the radio. They say: Here's a man dedicated to evil capable of enjoying the good. But what the imbecilic sods don't realize is that there

are two kinds of good – one neutral, outside ethics, purely aesthetic'" (*Testament*, p. 39). As I read it, however, *A Clockwork Orange* does not allow so easy a separation.

11 At least at this stage of his career; Nietzsche was later to turn against Wagner.

12 One might be tempted to see the contrast as one between heavenmetal and heavy metal, but heavy metal was not yet a genre in the early 1960s.

13 In their essay elsewhere in this volume, Gabbard and Sharma suggest that Kubrick's repertoire decisions were motivated by a desire to use "music that audiences were . . . likely to recognize" (ms. p. 97). That may well be true, but it's not a sufficient explanation of Kubrick's decision to move beyond the German canon, since there are plenty of recognizable hits even within the circumscribed limits of the Mozart-to-Orff tradition.

14 See, in this regard, Burgess's reported criticism of the rock score for the Royal Shakespeare production of his second dramatization as "Neo-wallpaper" (Hutchings, p. 46). See also Nehring's complaint that this musical distinction shows Burgess's antipathy to youth culture (90).

15 One distinction one might make here is between those scenes where the music is actually audible in the world of the characters and those scenes where it is heard only by the audience in the theater. For further discussion, see my "Rimsky and Salieri."

16 At the same time, this scene probably serves as a parody of the fight scenes in *West Side Story*.

17 This exempting of the tradition is furthered, in the film, by a curious shift in a plot detail. In the novel, the Ludovico technique makes Alex unable to listening to *any* of his favorite music, which suggests that whatever the problem is, it infects a large category of music. In the film, it's only the Ninth (which has been substituted for the Fifth in the Nazi soundtrack) that's affected – which suggests that the problem lies not in the German tradition or the way it is perceived, but simply in one piece's coincidental appearance under particular conditions.

BIBLIOGRAPHY

Austin, Charles M. "Stirring the Guttywuts." *The Christian Century* 89 (February 16, 1972): 207.

Beck, Bernard. "Violent Search for Heroism." *Society* 10 (November/December 1972): 39–47.

Booth, Wayne C. *The Company We Keep: An Ethics of Fiction*. Berkeley and Los Angeles: University of California Press, 1988.

Burgess, Anthony. *A Clockwork Orange*. New York: Ballantine Books, 1988.

Burgess, Anthony. *A Clockwork Orange: A Play with Music Based on His Novella of the Same Name*. London: Hutchinson, 1987.

Burgess, Anthony. *The Clockwork Testament or Enderby's End*. New York: Knopf, 1975.

Burgess, Jackson. "Reviews: *A Clockwork Orange*." *Film Quarterly* 25 (Spring 1972): 33–36.

Burke, Tom. "Malcolm McDowell: The Liberals, They Hate 'Clockwork.'" *New York Times*, 30 January 1972: Section 2: pp. 13 and 15.

Cain, James M. *Serenade*. In *Three by Cain*. New York: Vintage, 1989. 1–196.

Canby, Vincent. "*A Clockwork Orange* Dazzles the Senses and Mind." *New York Times*, 20 December 1971: 44.

Ciment, Michel. *Kubrick*. Trans. Gilbert Adair. New York: Holt, Rinehart and Winston, 1982.

Costello, Donald. P. "From Counter-Culture to Anti-Culture." *Commonweal* 96 (July 14, 1972): 383–386.

DeRosia, Margaret. "An Erotics of Violence: Masculinity and (Homo)Sexuality in Stanley Kubrick's *A Clockwork Orange*. In this volume.

Falsetto, Mario. *Stanley Kubrick: A Narrative and Stylistic Analysis*. Westport, CT: Praeger, 1994.

Gabbard, Krin, and Shailja Sharma. "Stanley Kubrick and the Art Cinema." In this volume.

Hanslick, Eduard. *The Beautiful in Music*. Trans. Gustav Cohen. Ed. Morris Weitz. Indianapolis: Bobbs-Merrill/Liberal Arts, 1957.

Hatch, Robert. "Films." *The Nation* 214 (January 3, 1972): 27–28.

Heckman, Don. "Soundtracks, Bon-Bons, Yip-ee-i-o's . . . and *A Clockwork Orange*." *New York Times*, 27 August 1972: Section 2, p. 20.

Houston, Penelope. "Film: Kubrick Country" (interview with Kubrick). *Saturday Review*, 25 December 1971: 42–44.

Hutchings, William. "'What's It Going To Be Then, Eh?': The Stage Odyssey of Anthony Burgess's *A Clockwork Orange*." *Modern Drama* 34 (March 1991): 34–48.

Kolker, Robert P. "A Clockwork Orange . . . Ticking." In this volume.

McClary, Susan. *Feminine Endings: Music, Gender, and Sexuality*. Minneapolis: University of Minnesota Press, 1991.

Nabokov, Vladimir. "Castle, Cloud, Lake." In *Nabokov's Dozen*. New York: Popular Library, 1958: 82–90.

Nelson, Thomas Allen. *Kubrick: Inside a Film Artist's Maze*. Bloomington: Indiana University Press, 2000.

Nehring, Neil. "The Shifting Relations of Literature and Popular Music in Postwar England." *Discourse* 12, no. 1 (Fall-Winter 1989–90): 78–103.

Proust, Marcel. *In Search of Lost Time: Volume I: Swann's Way*. Trans. C. K. Scott Moncrieff and Terence Kilmartin, rev. D. J. Enright. New York: The Modern Library, 1992.

Piston, Walter. *Harmony*. 3rd edition. New York: Norton, 1962.

Rabinowitz, Peter J. "Rimskii and Salieri." *O Rus!: Studia litteraria slavica in honorem Hugh McLean*. Simon Karlinsky, James L. Rice, and Barry P. Scherr, Eds. Berkeley: Berkeley Slavic Specialties, 1995. 57–66.

Rabinowitz, Peter J., and Jay Reise. "The Phonograph Behind the Door: Some Thoughts on Musical Literacy." *Reading World Literature: Theory, History, Practice*. Ed. Sarah Lawall. Austin: University of Texas Press, 1994: 287–308.

Tolstoy, Leo. *The Kreutzer Sonata*. Trans. Aylmer Maud. In *The Death of Ivan Ilych and Other Stories*. New York: Signet Classics, 1960: 157–239.

ROBERT HUGHES

The Décor of Tomorrow's Hell

Review in *Time*, December 27, 1971

Some movies are so inventive and powerful that they can be viewed again and again and each time yield up fresh illuminations. Stanley Kubrick's *A Clockwork Orange* is such a movie. Based on Anthony Burgess's 1963 novel of the same title, it is a merciless, demoniac satire of a near future terrorized by pathological teen-age toughs. When it opened last week, *Time* Movie Critic Jay Cocks hailed it as "chillingly and often hilariously believable." Below, *Time*'s art critic takes a further look at some of its aesthetic implications.

Stanley Kubrick's biting and dandyish vision of subtopia is not simply a social satire but a brilliant, cultural one. No movie in the last decade (perhaps in the history of film) has made such exquisitely chilling predictions about the future role of cultural artifacts – paintings, buildings, sculpture, music – in society, or extrapolated them from so undeceived a view of our present culture.

The time is somewhere in the next ten years; the police still wear Queen Elizabeth II's monogram on their caps and the politicians seem to be dressed by Blades and Mr. Fish. The settings have the glittery, spaced-out look of a Milanese design fair – all stamped Mylar and womb-form chairs, thick glass tables, brushed aluminum and chrome, sterile perspectives of unshuttered concrete and white molded plastic. The designed artifact is to *Orange* what technological gadgetry was to Kubrick's *2001*: a character in the drama, a mute and unblinking witness.

This alienating décor is full of works of art. Fiber-glass nudes, crouched like *Playboy* femlins in the Korova milk bar, serve as tables or dispense mescaline-laced milk from their nipples. They are, in fact, close parodies of the fetishistic furniture-sculpture of Allen Jones. The living room of the Cat Lady, whom Protagonist Alex (Malcolm Mc-Dowell) murders with an immense Arp-like sculpture of a phallus, is decked with the kind of garish, routinely erotic paintings that have infested Pop-art consciousness in recent years.

The impression, a very deliberate one, is of culture objects cut loose from any power to communicate, or even to be noticed. There is no reality to which they connect. Their owners possess them as so much paraphernalia, like the derby hats, codpieces and bleeding-eye emblems that Alex and his mates wear so defiantly on their bully-boy costumes. When Alex swats at the Cat Lady's sculptured *schlong*, she screams: "Leave that alone, don't touch it! It's a very important work of art!" This pathetic burst of connoisseur's jargon echoes in a vast cultural emptiness. In worlds like this, no work of art can be important.

The geography of Kubrick's bleak landscape becomes explicit in his use of music. Whenever the woodwinds and brass turn up on the sound track, one may be fairly sure that something atrocious will appear on the screen – and be distanced by the irony of juxtaposition. Thus to the strains of Rossini's *Thieving Magpie*, a girl is gang-raped in a deserted casino. In a sequence of exquisite *comédie noire*, Alex cripples a writer and rapes his wife while tripping through a Gene Kelly number: "Singin' in the rain" (*bash*), "Just singin' in the rain" (*kick*).

What might seem gratuitous is very pointed indeed. At issue is the popular 19th century idea, still held today, that Art is Good for You, that the purpose of the fine arts is to provide moral uplift. Kubrick's message, amplified from Burgess's novel, is the opposite: art has no ethical purpose. There is no religion of beauty. Art serves, instead, to promote ecstatic consciousness. The kind of ecstasy depends on the person who is having it. Without the slightest contradiction, Nazis could weep over Wagner before stoking the crematoriums. Alex grooves on the music of "Ludwig van," especially the Ninth Symphony, which fills him with fantasies of sex and slaughter.

When he is drug-cured of belligerence, strapped into a straitjacket with eyes clamped open to watch films of violence, the conditioning also works on his love of music. Beethoven makes him suicidal. Then, when the government returns him to his state of innocent viciousness, the love of Ludwig comes back: "I was really cured at last," he says over the last fantasy shot in which he is swiving a blonde amidst clapping Establishment figures in Ascot costume, while the mighty setting of Schiller's Ode to Joy peals on the soundtrack.

Kubrick delivers these insights with something of Alex's pure, consistent aggression. His visual style is swift and cold – appropriately, even necessarily so. Moreover, his direction has the rarest of qualities, bravura morality – ironic, precise and ferocious. "It's funny," muses Alex, "how the colors of the real world only seem really real when you viddy them on the screen." It is a good epigraph to *A Clockwork Orange*. No futures are inevitable, but little Alex, glaring through the false eyelashes that he affects while on his bashing rampages, rises from the joint imaginations of Kubrick and Burgess like a portent: he is the future Candide, not of innocence, but of excessive and frightful experience.

PAULINE KAEL

A Clockwork Orange: Stanley Strangelove

Review in *The New Yorker*, January 1, 1972

Literal-minded in its sex and brutality, Teutonic in its humor, Stanley Kubrick's *A Clockwork Orange* might be the work of a strict and exacting German professor who set out to make a porno-violent sci-fi comedy. Is there anything sadder – and ultimately more repellent – than a clean minded pornographer? The numerous rapes and beatings have no ferocity and no sensuality; they're frigidly, pedantically calculated, and because there is no motivating emotion, the viewer may experience them as an indignity and wish to leave. The movie follows the Anthony Burgess novel so closely that the book might have served as the script, yet that thick-skulled German professor may be Dr. Strangelove himself, because the meanings are turned around.

Burgess's 1962 novel is set in a vaguely Socialist future (roughly, the late seventies or early eighties) – in a dreary, routinized England that roving gangs of teen-age thugs terrorize at night. In perceiving the amoral destructive potential of youth gangs, Burgess's ironic fable differs from Orwell's *1984* in a way that already seems prophetically accurate. The novel is narrated by the leader of one of these gangs – Alex, a conscienceless schoolboy sadist – and, in a witty, extraordinarily sustained literary conceit, narrated in his own slang (Nadsat, the teen-agers' special dialect). The book is a fast read; Burgess, a composer turned novelist, has an ebullient, musical sense of language, and you pick up the meanings of the strange words as the prose rhythms speed you along. Alex enjoys stealing, stomping, raping, and destroying until he kills a woman and is sent to prison for fourteen years. After serving two, he arranges to get out by submitting to an experiment on conditioning, and he is turned into a moral robot who becomes nauseated at thoughts of sex and violence. Released when he is harmless, he falls prey to his former victims, who beat him and torment him until he attempts suicide. This leads to criticism of the government that robotized him – turned him into a clockwork orange – and he is deconditioned, becoming once again a thug, and now at loose and triumphant. The ironies are protean, but Burgess is clearly a humanist; his point of view is that of a Christian horrified by the possibilities of a society turned clockwork orange, in which life is so mechanized that men lose their capacity for moral choice. There seems to be no way in this boring, dehumanizing society for the boys to release their energies except in vandalism and crime; they do what they do as a matter of course. Alex the sadist is as mechanized a creature as Alex the good.

Stanley Kubrick's Alex (Malcolm McDowell) is not so much an expression of how this society has lost its soul as he is a force pitted against the society, and by making the victims of the thugs more repulsive and contemptible than the thugs, Kubrick has learned to love the punk sadist. The end is no longer the ironic triumph of a mechanized punk but a real triumph. Alex is the only likable person we see – his cynical bravado suggests a broad-nosed, working-class Olivier – and the movie puts us on his side. Alex, who gets kicks out of violence, is more alive than anybody else in the movie, and younger and more attractive, and McDowell plays him exuberantly, with the power and slyness of a young Cagney. Despite what Alex does at the beginning, McDowell makes you root for his foxiness, for his crookedness. For most of the movie, we see him tortured and beaten and humiliated, so when his bold, aggressive punk's nature is restored to him it seems not a joke on all of us but, rather, a victory in which we share, and Kubrick takes an exultant tone. The look in Alex's eyes at the end tells us that he isn't just a mechanized, choiceless sadist but prefers sadism and knows he can get by with it. Far from being a little parable about the dangers of soullessness and the horrors of force, whether employed by individuals against each other or by society in "conditioning," the movie becomes a vindication of Alex, saying that the punk was a free human being and only the good Alex was a robot.

The trick of making the attacked less human than their attackers, so you feel no sympathy for them, is, I think, symptomatic of a new attitude in movies. This attitude says there's no moral difference. Stanley Kubrick has assumed the deformed, self-righteous perspective of a vicious young punk who says, "Everything's rotten. Why shouldn't I do what I want? They're worse than I am." In the new mood (perhaps movies in their cumulative effect are partly responsible for it), people want to believe the hyperbolic worst, want to believe in the degradation of the victims – that they are dupes and phonies and weaklings. I can't accept that Kubrick is merely reflecting this post-assassinations, post-Manson mood; I think he's catering to it. I think he wants to dig it.

This picture plays with violence in an intellectually seductive way. And though it has no depth, it's done in such a slow, heavy style that those prepared to like it can treat its puzzling aspects as oracular. It can easily be construed as an ambiguous mystery play, a visionary warning against "the Establishment." There are a million ways to justify identifying with Alex: Alex is fighting repression; he's alone against the system. What he does isn't nearly as bad as what the government does (both in the movie and in the United States now). Why shouldn't he be violent? That's all the Establishment has ever taught him (and us) to be. The point of the book was that we must be as men, that we must be able to take responsibility for what we are. The point of the movie is much more *au courant*. Kubrick has removed many of the obstacles to our identifying with Alex; the Alex of the book has had his personal habits cleaned up a bit – his fondness for squishing small animals under his tires, his taste for ten-year-old girls, his beating up of other prisoners, and so on. And Kubrick aids the identification with Alex by small directorial choices throughout. The writer whom Alex cripples (Patrick Magee) and the woman he kills are cartoon nasties with upper-class accents a mile wide. (Magee has been encouraged to act like a bathetic madman; he seems to be preparing for a career in horror movies.) Burgess gave us society through Alex's eyes, and so the vision was deformed, and Kubrick, carrying over from *Dr. Strangelove* his joky adolescent view of hypocritical, sexually dirty authority figures and extending it to all adults, has added an extra layer of deformity. The "straight" people are far more twisted than Alex; they seem inhuman and incapable of suffering. He alone suffers. And how he suffers! He's a male Little Nell – screaming in a straitjacket during the brainwashing; sweet and helpless when rejected by his parents; alone, weeping, on a bridge; beaten, bleeding, lost in a rainstorm; pounding his head on a floor and crying for death. Kubrick pours on the hearts and flowers; what is done to Alex is far worse than what Alex has done, so society itself can be felt to justify Alex's hoodlumism.

The movie's confusing – and, finally, corrupt – morality is not, however, what makes it such an abhorrent viewing experience. It is offensive long before one perceives where it is heading, because it has no shadings. Kubrick, a director with an arctic spirit, is determined to be pornographic, and he has no talent for it. In *Los Olvidados*, Buñuel showed teen-agers committing horrible brutalities, and even though you had no illusions about their victims – one, in particular, was a foul old lecher – you were appalled. Buñuel makes you understand the pornography of brutality: the pornography is in what human beings are capable of doing to other human beings. Kubrick has always been one of the least sensual and least erotic of directors, and his attempts here at phallic humor are like a professor's lead balloons. He tries to work up kicky violent scenes, carefully estranging you from the victims so that you can enjoy the rapes and beatings. But I think one is more likely to feel cold antipathy toward the movie than horror at the violence – or enjoyment of it, either.

Kubrick's martinet control is obvious in the terrible performances he gets from everybody but McDowell, and in the inexorable pacing. The film has a distinctive style of estrangement: gloating closeups, bright, hard-edge, third-degree lighting, and abnormally loud voices. It's a style, all right – the movie doesn't look like other movies, or sound like them – but it's a leering, portentous style. After the balletic brawling of the teen-age gangs, with bodies flying as in a Western saloon fight, and after the gang-bang of the writer's wife and an orgy in speeded-up motion, you're primed for more action, but you're left stranded in the prison sections, trying to find some humor in tired schoolboy jokes about a Hitlerian guard. The movie retains a little of the slangy Nadsat but none of the fast rhythms of Burgess's prose, and so the dialect seems much more arch than it does in the book. Many of the dialogue sequences go on and on, into a stupor of inactivity. Kubrick seems infatuated with the hypnotic possibilities of static setups; at times you feel as if you were trapped in front of the frames of a comic strip for a numbing ten minutes per frame. When Alex's correctional officer visits his home and he and Alex sit on a bed, the camera sits on the two of them. When Alex comes home from prison, his parents and the lodger who has displaced him are in the living room; Alex appeals to his seated, unloving parents for an inert eternity. Long after we've got the point, the composition is still telling us to appreciate its cleverness. This ponderous technique is hardly leavened by the structural use of classical music to characterize the sequences; each sequence is scored to Purcell (synthesized on a Moog), Rossini, or Beethoven, while Elgar and others are used for brief satiric effects. In the book, the doctor who has devised the conditioning treatment explains why the horror images used in it are set to music: "It's a useful emotional heightener." But the whole damned movie is heightened this way; yes, the music is effective, but the effect is self-important.

When I pass a newsstand and see the saintly, bearded, intellectual Kubrick on the cover of *Saturday Review*, I wonder: Do people notice things like the way Kubrick cuts to the rival teen-age gang before Alex and his hoods arrive to fight them, just so we can have the pleasure of watching that gang strip the struggling girl they mean to rape? Alex's voice is on the track announcing his arrival, but Kubrick can't wait for Alex to arrive, because then he couldn't show us as much. That girl is stripped for our benefit; it's the purest exploitation. Yet this film lusts for greatness, and I'm not sure that Kubrick knows how to make simple movies anymore, or that he cares to, either. I don't know how consciously he has thrown this film to youth. Maybe he's more of a showman than he lets on – a lucky showman with opportunism built into the cells of his body. The film can work at a pop-fantasy level for a young audience already prepared to accept Alex's view of the society, ready to believe that that's how it is.

At the movies, we are gradually being conditioned to accept violence as a sensual pleasure. The directors used to say they were showing us its real face and how ugly it was in order to sensitize us to its horrors. You don't have to be very keen to see that they are now in fact desensitizing us. They are saying that everyone is brutal, and the heroes must be as brutal as the villains or they turn into fools. There seems to be an assumption that if you're offended by movie brutality,

you are somehow playing into the hands of the people who want censorship. But this would deny those of us who don't believe in censorship the use of the only counterbalance: the freedom of the press
to say that there's anything conceivably damaging in these films –
the freedom to analyze their implications. If we don't use this critical freedom, we are implicitly saying that no brutality is too much
for us – that only squares and people who believe in censorship are
concerned with brutality. Actually, those who believe in censorship
are primarily concerned with sex, and they generally worry about violence only when it's eroticized. This means that practically no one
raises the issue of the possible cumulative effects of movie brutality.
Yet surely, when night after night atrocities are served up to us as entertainment, it's worth some anxiety. We become clockwork oranges
if we accept all this pop culture without asking what's in it. How can
people go on talking about the dazzling brilliance of movies and not
notice that the directors are sucking up to the thugs in the audience?

A Glossary of Nadsat

An early glossary was created by Stanley Edgar Hyman, assisted by "the kindness" of his colleague Nora Montesinos and "a number of correspondents." The glossary and an "Afterward" also by Stanley Edgar Hyman were printed in the Ballantine Books paperback edition (1965) of the novel. Burgess was strongly opposed to such aids, feeling that readers should learn the language in the course of reading his novel. However, there are now a number of glossaries of nadsat on the Web. I have built upon Hyman's work as well as the Web sites. I have also drawn on my experience in teaching this novel over a number of years to expand existing versions of the glossary. My colleague at Macalaster College, Gitta Hammarberg, has provided transliterations of the Russian etymologies using a modified version of the Library of Congress system (modified in that diacritics are omitted) outlined by J. Thomas Shaw in *The Transliteration of Modern Russian for English-Language Publications* (1967) and has corrected and expanded the glossary further.

appy polly loggy	apology (childhood slang)
baboochka	old woman (Russian: babushka/grandmother)
baddiwad	bad (childhood slang)
banda	band (Russian: banda/band, gang)
barbering	haircut (invented slang)
barry places	jail cells (invented slang)
bellpush	door bell (invented slang)
biblio	library (Russian: biblioteka/library)

bezoomny	mad (Russian: bezumnyi/mad, insane)
bitva	battle (Russian: bitva/battle)
Bog	God (Russian: Bog/God)
bolnoy	sick (Russian: bol'noi/sick)
bolshy	big, great (Russian: bol'shoi/big)
brat, bratty	brother (Russian: brat/brother)
bratchny	bastard (Russian: vnebrachnyi/illegitimate)
bruiseboys	bouncers, bodyguards (invented slang)
britva	razor (Russian: britva/razor)
brooko	belly (Russian: bryukho/belly)
brosat	to throw (Russian: brosat'/to throw)
bugatty	rich (Russian: bogatyi/wealthy)
burble	to utter nonsense (invented slang)
cables	arteries (Russian: kabel/electric cables)
cal	feces (Russian: kal/excrement, feces)
cancer	cigarette (invented slang)
cantora	office (Russian: kontora/office)
carman	pocket (Russian: karman/pocket)
chai	tea (Russian: chai/tea)
charles, charlie	chaplain (invented slang [backformation from Charlie Chaplin])
chasha	cup (Russian: chashka/cup)
chasso	guard (Russian: chasovoi/sentry)
cheena	woman (Russian: zhenshchina/woman)
cheest	to wash (Russian: chistit'/to clean)
chelloveck	person, man, fellow (Russian: chelovek/person, man)
chepooka	nonsense (Russian: chepukha/nonsense)
choodessny	wonderful (Russian: chudesnyi/miraculous)
chumble	to mumble (invented slang: chatter + mumble)
clop	to bang (Russian: khlopat'/flap, slam, bang and khlop/bang!)
cluve	beak (Russian: kliuv/beak)
collocoll	bell (Russian: kolokol/bell)
crack	to break up or "bust" (invented slang)
crast	to steal or rob; robbery (Russian: krast'/steal)
creech	to shout or scream (Russian: krichat'/scream)
cubie	cubicle, room (Russian: cub/cube; rooms are often measured in cubic meters in Russia)
cutter	money (invented slang)

dama	lady (Russian: dama/lady)
decreps	old people (invented slang from "decrepit")
ded	old man (Russian: ded/grandfather)
deng	money (Russian: den'gi/money)
devotchka	girl (Russian: devochka/girl)
disc-bootik	record store (invented slang)
dobby	good (Russian: dobryi/good)
domy	house (Russian: dom/house)
doobidoob	goodie-good (invented slang)
dook	trace, ghost (Russian: dukh/spirit, ghost, breath)
dorogoy	dear, valuable (Russian: dorogoi/expensive, dear)
drat	fight (Russian: drat'sia/to fight; drat'/to tear, to flog, to fleece)
drencrom	drug (invented slang)
droog	friend (Russian: drug/friend)
dung	to defecate (invented slang)
dva	two (Russian: dva/two)
eegra	game (Russian: igra/game)
eemya	name (Russian: imia/name)
eggiweg	egg (childhood slang)
fashed	exhausted (invented slang)
filly	to play or fool with (invented slang)
firegold	drink (invented slang)
fist	to punch (invented slang)
flip	wild (?)
forella	trout (Russian: forel/trout)
gazetta	newspaper (Russian: gazeta/newspaper)
gets	a term of insult (invented slang)
glazz	eye (Russian: glaz/eye)
gloopy	stupid (Russian: glupyi/foolish, stupid)
godman	priest (invented slang: man of God)
golly	unit of money (invented slang [related to lolly/money])
goloss	voice (Russian: golos/voice)
goober	lip (Russian: guba/lip)
gooly	to walk (Russian: guliat'/to walk, stroll)
gorlo	throat (Russian: gorlo/throat)
govoreet	to speak or talk (Russian: govorit'/to speak)
grahzny	dirty (Russian: griaznyi/dirty)
grazzy	soiled (Russian: griaznyi/dirty)

gromky	loud (Russian: gromkii/loud)
groody	breast (Russian: grud'/breast)
gruppa	group (Russian: gruppa/group)
guff	laugh (invented slang from "guffaw")
gulliver	head (Russian: golova/head)
guttiwuts	guts (childhood slang)
hen-korm	chickenfeed (Russian: kormit/to feed; korm/feed, fodder)
horn	to cry out, yell (invented slang: sound a horn)
horrorshow	good, well (Russian: khorosho/good)
hound and horny	corny (invented slang)
in-out in-out	sexual intercourse (invented slang)
interessovat	to interest (Russian: interesovat'/to interest)
itty	to go (Russian: idti/to go)
jammiwam	jam (childhood slang)
jeezny	life (Russian: zhizn'/life)
jelly mold	codpiece (invented slang)
kartoffel	potato (Russian: kartofel'/potatoes)
keeshkas	guts (Russian: kishka/intestines)
kleb	bread (Russian: khleb/bread)
klootch	key (Russian: kliuch/key)
knives	a drug to make one violent (invented slang)
knopka	button (Russian: knopka/push-button)
kopat	to "dig" [1960s slang] (Russian: kopat'/to dig [a hole, etc.])
koshka	cat (Russian: koshka/cat)
kot	tomcat (Russian: kot/kat)
krovvy	blood (Russian: krov'/blood)
kupet	to buy (Russian: kupit'/to buy)
land	"in the land," high, intoxicated; "out of the land," sobering up (invented slang)
lapa	paw (Russian: lapa/paw)
lewdies	people (Russian: liudi/people)
lighter	crone (invented slang, related to blighter?)
litso	face (Russian: litso/face)
lomtick	piece, bit (Russian: lomtik/slice [of bread])
lovet	catch (Russian: lovit'/to catch)
lubbilubbing	making love (Russian: liubit'/to love; liubov'/love)
lucious glory	hair (invented slang)

luna	moon (Russian: luna/moon)
malchick	boy (Russian: mal'chik/boy)
malenky	little, tiny (Russian: malen'kii/small)
mappy	lined, creased (slang)
maslo	butter (Russian: maslo/butter)
merzky	filthy (Russian: merzkii/loathsome, vile)
messel	thought, fancy (Russian: mysl'/thought)
mesto	place (Russian: mesto/place)
millicent	policeman (Russian: militsiia/militia, police; militsioner/militia man)
minoota	minute (Russian: minuta/minute)
molodoy	young (Russian: molodoi/young)
moloko	milk (Russian: moloko/milk)
moodge	man (Russian: muzhchina/man)
morder	nose, snout (Russian: morda/snout)
mounch	snack (invented slang, from "munch")
mozg	brain (Russian: mozg/brain)
nachinat	to begin (Russian: nachinat'/to begin)
nadmenny	arrogant (Russian: nadmennyi/arrogant)
nadsat	teen (Russian ending for numbers 11–19)
nagoy	naked (Russian: nagoi/naked)
nazz	fool (Russian: nazad/literally backwards, ago)
neezhnies	underpants (Russian: nizhnyi/lower)
nochy	night (Russian: noch'/night)
noga	leg, foot (Russian: noga/foot)
nozh	knife (Russian: nozh/knife)
nuke	smell (Russian: niukhat'/to smell)
oddy knocky	lonesome (Russian: odinokii/lonesome)
odin	one (Russian: odin/one)
okno	window (Russian: okno/window)
oobivat	to kill (Russian: ubivat'/to kill)
ookadeet	to leave (Russian: ukhodit'/to leave)
ooko	ear (Russian: ukho/ear)
oomny	clever (Russian: umnyi/clever)
oozhassny	terrible (Russian: uzhasnyi/terrible)
oozy	chain (Russian: uzh/snake)
osoosh	to wipe, dry (Russian: osushat'/to dry)
otchkies	eyeglasses (Russian: ochki/glasses)
pan-handle	erection (invented slang)

pantalonies	pants (Russian: pantalony/pants, trousers)
pee and em	parents (invented slang, from papa [p] and mum [m])
peet	to drink (Russian: pit'/to drink)
pishcha	food (Russian: pishcha/food)
platch	to cry (Russian: plakat'/to cry)
platties	clothes (Russian: plat'e/clothes)
plenny	prisoner (Russian: plennyi/prisoner)
plesk	splash (Russian: pleskat'/to splash)
pletcho	shoulder (Russian: plecho/shoulder)
plott	body (Russian: plot'/flesh)
podooshka	pillow (Russian: podushka/pillow)
pol	sex (Russian: pol/sex, gender)
polezny	useful (Russian: poleznyi/useful)
polyclef	skeleton key (invented slang: poly/many = clef/key)
pony	to understand (Russian: ponimat'/to understand)
poog	fright (Russian: pugat'/to frighten)
poogly	frightened (Russian: pugat'/to frighten)
pooshka	gun, cannon (Russian: pushka/cannon)
popdisc	album (invented slang)
prestoopnik	criminal (Russian: prestupnik/criminal)
pretty polly	money (slang derived from "lolly"/money)
privodeet	to lead somewhere (Russian: privodit'/to bring, to lead)
prod	to produce (invented slang)
ptitsa	"chick," "bird," [1960s slang for girl] (Russian: ptitsa/bird)
pyahnitsa	drunk (Russian: pianitsa/drunkard)
rabbit	work, job (Russian: rabota/work)
radosty	joy (Russian: radost'/joy)
raskazz	story (Russian: rasskaz/story)
rassoodock	mind (Russian: rassudok/sanity)
raz	time (Russian: raz/occasion, time)
razdraz	upset (Russian: razdrazhat'/to irritate)
razrez	to rip, ripping (Russian: razrezat'/to cut, to rip; razrez/cut, section)
rook, rooker	hand (and rarely, arm) (Russian: ruka/hand)

rot	mouth (Russian: rot/mouth)
rozz	cop, policeman (Russian: rozha/ugly face, mug)
rozz-shop	police station (invented slang [see "rozz"])
sabog	shoe (Russian: sapog/boot, tall shoe)
sakar	sugar (Russian: sakhar/sugar)
sammy	generous (Russian: samyi/the most)
sarky	sarcastic (invented slang)
scoteena	beast (Russian: skotina/brute, beast)
shaika	gang (Russian: shaika/gang, of thieves)
sharp	woman (invented slang)
sharries	testicles (Russian: shar/ball, sphere; shariki/marbles)
shest	pole (Russian: pole, staff)
sick up	to vomit (invented slang)
sidlers	those who sidle up (invented slang)
shilarny	concern (invented slang)
shive	slice (invented slang)
shiyah	neck (Russian: sheia/neck)
shlaga	club (German: Schläger/club, bat)
shlapa	hat (Russian: shliapa/hat)
shlem	helmet (Russian: shlem/helmet)
shoom	noise (Russian: shum/noise)
shoot	fool (Russian: shut/fool, jester)
sinny	movies (invented slang from cinema)
sizy	grey/blue (Russian: blue-grey, dove blue color)
skazat	to say (Russian: skazat'/to say)
skolliwoll	school (childhood slang)
skorry	quick, quickly (Russian: skorii/quick)
skrike	scratch (invented slang from strike + scratch)
skvat	to grab (Russian: khvatat'/to grab, snatch)
sladky	sweet (Russian: sladkii/sweet)
sloochat	to happen (Russian: sluchat'sia/to happen)
sloosh, slooshy	to hear, to listen (Russian: slushat'/to hear)
slop	time meal time (invented slang)
slovo	word (Russian: slovo/word)
smeck	laugh (Russian: smekh/laughter, laugh)
smot	to look (Russian: smotret'/to look)
sneety	dream (Russian: snit'sia/to dream)
snoutie	tobacco [snuff] (invented slang)
snuff it	to die (slang, "to snuff" is "to kill")

sobirat	to pick up (Russian: sobirat'/to gather)
sod	to fornicate, fornicator (slang from sodomy/sodomite)
soomka	"bag" [1960s slang for old woman] (Russian: sumka/bag)
soviet	advice, order (Russian: sovet/advice, council)
spat	to sleep (Russian: spat'/to sleep)
spatchka	sleep (Russian: spat'/to sleep)
split	to gossip (Russian: spletnichat/ to gossip, talk scandal)
splooge, splosh	splash (invented slang)
spoogy	terrified (Russian: spugivat'/to frighten)
Staja	State Jail (invented slang)
starry	ancient (Russian: staryi/old)
strack	horror (Russian: strakh/fear)
synthemesc	drug (invented slang [synthetic mescaline])
tally	waist (Russian: talia/waist)
tashtook	handkerchief (German: taschentuch/handkerchief)
tass	cup (French: tasse/cup)
ticklewickle	to tickle (invented slang)
tolchock	to hit or push; blow, beating (Russian: tolchok/push, shove)
toofle	slipper (Russian: tuflia/shoe, slipper)
tree	three (Russian: tri/three)
twenty-to-one	sexual violence (invented slang)
twitters	bird sounds (invented slang)
unplatty	to undress (Russian: plat'e' [noun], dress, clothes, clothing)
Up-your-piping	up yours (vulgar gesture) (invented slang)
vareet	to "cook up," plan (Russian: varit'/to cook up)
vaysay	washroom (invented slang from French pronunciation of W.C. [water closet])
veck	(see chelloveck)
vellocet	drug (invented slang)
veshch	thing (Russian: veshch'/thing)
viddy	to see or look (Russian: videt'/to see)
voloss	hair (Russian: volos/hair)
von	smell (Russian: von/stench)
vred	to harm or damage (Russian: vred/to harm)

warble	song (invented slang)
yahma	hole (Russian: iama/hole, pit)
yahoodies	Jews (invented slang)
yahzick	tongue (Russian: iazik/tongue)
yarbles	testicles (invented slang)
yawp	mouth (slang)
yeckate	to drive (Russian: ekhat'/to go)
zammechat	remarkable (Russian: zamechatelnyi/remarkable)
zasnoot	sleep (Russian: zasnut'/to fall asleep)
zheena	wife (Russian: zhena/wife)
zoobies	teeth (Russian: zubi/teeth)
zvonock	doorbell (Russian: zvonok/doorbell)
zvook	sound (Russian: zvuk/sound)

Filmography

1951

DAY OF THE FIGHT
SCRIPT: Robert Rein
DIRECTOR, PHOTOGRAPHY, EDITING, SOUND: Stanley Kubrick
MUSIC: Gerald Fried
COMMENTARY: Douglas Edwards
PRODUCER: Jay Bonafield
DISTRIBUTOR: RKO Radio
LENGTH: 16 minutes. Black-and-white

1951

FLYING PADRE
DIRECTOR, PHOTOGRAPHY, EDITING, SOUND: Stanley Kubrick
MUSIC: Nathaniel Shilkret
NARRATOR: Bob Hite
PRODUCER: Burton Benjamin
DISTRIBUTOR: RKO Radio
LENGTH: 8 minutes, 30 seconds. Black-and-white

1953

THE SEAFARERS
SCRIPT: Will Chasan
DIRECTOR, PHOTOGRAPHY,: Stanley Kubrick
NARRATOR: Don Hollenbeck

PRODUCER: Lester Cooper
DISTRIBUTOR: Seafarers International Union, Atlantic
    and Gulf Coast, AFL
LENGTH: 30 minutes. Color

FEAR AND DESIRE
SCRIPT: Howard O. Sackler
DIRECTOR, PHOTOGRAPHY, EDITOR: Stanley Kubrick
MUSIC: Gerald Fried
PRODUCER: Stanley Kubrick
PRODUCTION COMPANY: Stanley Kubrick Productions
DISTRIBUTOR: Joseph Burstyn
CAST: Frank Silvera (Mac), Kenneth Harp (Corby/General), Virginia
    Leith (The Girl), Paul Mazursky (Sidney), Steve Coit (Fletcher/aide),
    David Allen (Narrator)
LENGTH: 68 minutes. Black-and-white

1955

KILLER'S KISS
SCRIPT: Stanley Kubrick, Howard O. Sackler
DIRECTOR: Photography, Editor, Stanley Kubrick
MUSIC: Gerald Fried
CHOREOGRAPHY: David Vaughan
PRODUCERS: Stanley Kubrick, Morris Bousel
PRODUCTION: Company: Minotaur
DISTRIBUTOR: United Artists
CAST: Frank Silvera (Vincent Rapallo), Jamie Smith (Davy Gordon),
    Irene Kane (Gloria Price), Jerry Jarret (Albert), Ruth Sobotka (Iris),
    Mike Dana, Felice Orlandi, Ralph Roberts, Phil Stevenson (Gangsters),
    Skippy Adelman (Mannequin Factory Owner), David Vaughan, Alec
    Rubin (Conventioneers), Shaun O'Brien, Barbara Brand, Arthur
    Fedelman, Bill Funaro
LENGTH: 67 minutes. Black-and-white

1956

THE KILLING
SCRIPT: Stanley Kubrick. Based on the novel *Clean Break*, by Lionel
    White. Additional dialogue, Jim Thompson
DIRECTOR: Stanley Kubrick

PHOTOGRAPHY: Lucien Ballard
EDITOR: Betty Steinberg
ART DIRECTOR: Ruth Sobotka
SOUND: Earl Snyder
MUSIC: Gerald Fried
PRODUCER: James B. Harris
PRODUCTION COMPANY: Harris–Kubrick Productions
DISTRIBUTOR: United Artists
CAST: Sterling Hayden (Johnny Clay), Jay C. Flippen (Marvin Unger), Marie Windsor (Sherry Peatty), Elisha Cook, Jr. (George Peatty), Coleen Gray (Fay), Vince Edwards (Val Cannon), Ted DeCorsia (Randy Kennan), Joe Sawyer (Mike O'Reilly), Timothy Carey (Nikki Arane), Kola Kwariani (Maurice Oboukhoff), James Edwards (Parking Lot Attendant), Jay Adler (Leo), Joseph Turkel (Tiny), Tito Vuolo, Dorothy Adams, Herbert Ellis, James Griffith, Cecil Elliot, Steve Mitchell, Mary Carroll, William Benedict, Charles R. Cane, Robert B. Williams
LENGTH: 83 minutes. Black-and-white

1957

PATHS OF GLORY
SCRIPT: Stanley Kubrick, Calder Willingham, Jim Thompson, based on the novel by Humphrey Cobb
DIRECTOR: Stanley Kubrick
PHOTOGRAPHY: George Krause
EDITOR: Eva Kroll
ART DIRECTOR: Ludwig Reiber
MUSIC: Gerald Fried
SOUND: Martin Muller
PRODUCER: James B. Harris
PRODUCTION COMPANY: Harris–Kubrick Productions
DISTRIBUTOR: United Artists
CAST: Kirk Douglas (Colonel Dax), Ralph Meeker (Corporal Paris), Adolphe Menjou (General Broulard), George Macready (General Mireau), Wayne Morris (Lieutenant Roget), Richard Anderson (Major Saint-Auban), Joseph Turkel (Private Arnaud), Timothy Carey (Private Ferol), Peter Capell (Judge), Susanne Christian (Young German Girl), Bert Freed (Sergeant Boulanger), Emile Meyer (Priest), Jerry Hausner (Meyer), Fred Bell (Wounded Soldier), Harold Benedict (Sargeant Nichols), John Stein (Captain Rousseau), Ken Dibbs (Lejeune)
LENGTH: 86 minutes. Black-and-white

1960

SPARTACUS

SCRIPT: Dalton Trumbo, based on the novel by Howard Fast
DIRECTOR: Stanley Kubrick
PHOTOGRAPHY: Russell Metty
ADDITIONAL PHOTOGRAPHY: Clifford Stine
EDITORS: Robert Lawrence, Robert Schulte, Fred Chulack
PRODUCTION DESIGNER: Alexander Golitzen
ART DIRECTOR: Eric Orbom
SET DECORATION: Russell A. Gausman, Julia Heron
TITLES: Saul Bass
TECHNICAL ADVISER: Vittorio Nino Novarese
MUSIC: Alex North
MUSIC DIRECTOR: Joseph Gershenson
SOUND: Waldon O. Watson, Joe Lapis, Murray Spivack, Ronald Pierce
EXECUTIVE PRODUCER: Kirk Douglas
PRODUCER: Edward Lewis
PRODUCTION COMPANY: Byna Productions, Inc.
DISTRIBUTOR: Universal International
CAST: Kirk Douglas (Spartacus), Laurence Olivier (Marcus Crassus), Jean
    Simmons (Varinia), Charles Laughton (Gracchus), Peter Ustinov
    (Lentulus Batiatus), John Gavin (Julius Caesar), Tony Curtis
    (Antoninus), Nina Foch (Helena), Herbert Lom (Tigranes), John
    Ireland (Crixus), John Dall (Glabrus), Charles McGraw (Marcellus),
    Joanna Barnes (Claudia), Harold J. Stone (David), Woody Strode
    (Draba), Peter Brocco (Ramon), Paul Lambert (Gannicus), Robert J.
    Wilke (Captain of the Guard), Nicholas Dennis (Dionysius), John
    Hoyt (Roman Officer), Frederic Worlock (Laelius), Dayton Lummis
    (Symmachus), Jill Jarmyn, Jo Summers
ORIGINAL RUNNING TIME: 196 minutes. Technicolor
(Note: The running time of the film shown in Britain was three min-
utes shorter. Later, when the film was in general distribution, Uni-
versal cut it to 184 minutes for all countries and subsequent releases.
The restored version [1992] is 196 minutes.)

1962

LOLITA

SCRIPT: Vladimir Nabokov, based on his own novel
DIRECTOR: Stanley Kubrick

PHOTOGRAPHY: Oswald Morris
EDITOR: Anthony Harvey
ART DIRECTOR: Bill Andrews
MUSIC: Nelson Riddle
LOLITA THEME MUSIC: Bob Harris
SOUND: H. L. Bird, Len Shilton
PRODUCER: James B. Harris
PRODUCTION COMPANY: Seven Arts /Anya /Transworld
DISTRIBUTOR: Metro-Goldwyn-Mayer
CAST: James Mason (Humbert Humbert), Sue Lyon (Lolita), Shelley
    Winters (Charlotte Haze), Peter Sellers (Clare Quilty), Diana Decker
    (Jean Farlow), Jerry Stovin (John Farlow), Suzanne Gibbs (Mona
    Farlow), Gary Cockrell (Dick), Marianne Stone (Vivian Darkbloom),
    Cec Linder (Physician), Lois Maxwell (Nurse Mary Lore), William
    Greene (George Swine), C. Denier Warren (Potts), Isobel Lucas
    (Louise), Maxine Holden (Hospital Receptionist), James Dyrenforth
    (Beale), Roberta Shore (Lorna), Eric Lane (Roy), Shirley Douglas
    (Mrs. Starch), Roland Brand (Bill), Colin Maitland (Charlie), Irvin
    Allen (Hospital Intern), Marion Mathie (Miss Lebone), Craig Sams
    (Rex), John Harrison (Tom), Terence Kilburn
RUNNING TIME: 152 minutes. Black-and-white

1964

DR. STRANGELOVE OR: HOW I LEARNED TO STOP WORRYING AND LOVE THE BOMB

SCRIPT: Stanley Kubrick, Terry Southern, Peter George, based on the
    novel *Red Alert*, by Peter George
DIRECTOR: Stanley Kubrick
PHOTOGRAPHY: Gilbert Taylor
EDITOR: Anthony Harvey
PRODUCTION DESIGNER: Ken Adam
ART DIRECTOR: Peter Murton
SPECIAL EFFECTS: Wally Veevers
MUSIC: Laurie Johnson
AVIATION ADVISER: Captain John Crewdson
SOUND: John Cox
PRODUCER: Stanley Kubrick
ASSOCIATE PRODUCER: Victor Lyndon
PRODUCTION COMPANY: Hawk Films Ltd.
DISTRIBUTOR: Columbia Pictures

CAST: Peter Sellers (Group Captain Lionel Mandrake, President Muffley, Dr. Strangelove), George C. Scott (General "Buck" Turgidson), Sterling Hayden (General Jack D. Ripper), Keenan Wynn (Colonel "Bat" Guano), Slim Pickens (Major T. J. "King" Kong), Peter Bull (Ambassador de Sadesky), Tracy Reed (Miss Scott), James Earl Jones (Lieutenant Lothar Zogg), Jack Creley (Mr. Staines), Frank Berry (Lieutenant H. R. Dietrich), Glen Beck (Lieutenant W. D. Kival), Shane Rimmer (Captain G. A. "Ace" Owens), Paul Tamarin (Lieutenant B. Goldberg, Radio Operator), Gordon Tanner (General Faceman), Robert O'Neil (Admiral Randolph), Roy Stephens (Frank), Laurence Herder, John McCarthy, Hal Galili (Members of Burpelson Base Defense Corps)
RUNNING TIME: 93 minutes. Black-and-white

1968

2001: A SPACE ODYSSEY

SCRIPT: Stanley Kubrick, Arthur C. Clarke, based on the latter's short story "The Sentinel"
DIRECTOR: Stanley Kubrick
PHOTOGRAPHY: Geoffrey Unsworth
ADDITIONAL PHOTOGRAPHY: John Alcott
EDITOR: Ray Lovejoy
ART DIRECTOR: John Hoesli
PRODUCTION DESIGNERS: Tony Masters, Harry Lange, Ernie Archer
  Special Photographic Effects Supervisors: Wally Veevers, Douglas Trumbull, Con Pederson, Tom Howard
SOUND: Winston Ryder
MUSIC: Richard Strauss, Johann Strauss, Aram Khachaturian, György Ligeti
PRODUCER: Stanley Kubrick
PRODUCTION COMPANY: Metro-Goldwyn-Mayer
DISTRIBUTOR: Metro-Goldwyn Mayer
CAST: Keir Dullea (David Bowman), Gary Lockwood (Frank Poole), William Sylvester (Dr. Heywood Floyd), Daniel Richter (Moon-watcher), Douglas Rain (Voice of HAL 9000), Leonard Rossiter (Smyslov), Margaret Tyzack (Elena), Robert Beatty (Halvorsen), Sean Sullivan (Michaels), Frank Miller (Mission Controller), Penny Brahms (Stewardess), Alan Gifford (Poole's Father), Vivian Kubrick (Dr. Floyd's daughter), Bill Weston, Edward Bishop, Glenn Beck, Edwina Carroll, Heather Downham, Mike Lovell, Peter Delmar,

Danny Grover, Brian Hawley, Ann Gillis, John Ashley, Peter Delmar,
David Hines, Darryl Paes, Jimmy Bell, Terry Duggan, Tony Jackson,
Joe Refalo, David Charkham, David Fleetwood, John Jordan, Andy
Wallace, Simon Davis, Danny Grover, Scott Mackee, Bob Wilyman,
Jonathan Daw, Brian Hawley, Laurence Marchant, Richard Wood
RUNNING TIME: 139 Minutes. Color
(Note: The original running time of *2001: A Space Odyssey*, when
previewed on April 1, 1968, in New York, was 161 minutes. Kubrick
subsequently decided to cut it by 22 minutes.)

1971

A CLOCKWORK ORANGE
SCRIPT: Stanley Kubrick, based on the novel by Anthony Burgess
DIRECTOR: Stanley Kubrick
PHOTOGRAPHY: John Alcott
EDITOR: Bill Butler
PRODUCTION DESIGNER: John Barry
SPECIAL PAINTINGS AND SCULPTURE: Herman Makkink, Cornelius
    Makkink, Liz Moore, Christiane Kubrick
ART DIRECTORS: Russell Hagg, Peter Shields
SOUND: Brian Blamey
ELECTRONIC MUSIC: Walter Carlos
MUSIC: Henry Purcell, Gioacchino Rossini, Ludwig van Beethoven,
    Nikolai Rimsky-Korsakov, Arthur Freed and Nacio Herb Brown,
    Sir Edward Elgar, Terry Tucker, Erika Eigen
EXECUTIVE PRODUCERS: Max L. Raab, Si Litvinoff
ASSOCIATE PRODUCER: Bernard Williams
PRODUCER: Stanley Kubrick
PRODUCTION COMPANY: Warner Bros. /Hawk Films
DISTRIBUTOR: Warner Bros.
CAST: Malcolm McDowell (Alex), Patrick Magee (Mr. Alexander),
    Michael Bates (Chief Guard), Warren Clarke (Dim), John Clive (Stage
    Actor), Adrienne Corri (Mrs. Alexander), Carl Duering (Dr. Brodsky),
    Paul Farrell (Tramp), Clive Francis (Lodger), Michael Gover (Prison
    Governor), Miriam Karlin (Cat Lady), James Marcus (Georgie), Aubrey
    Morris (P. R. Deltoid), Godfrey Quigley (Prison Chaplain), Sheila
    Raynor (Mum), Madge Ryan (Dr. Branom), John Savident
    (Conspirator), Anthony Sharp (Minister of the Interior), Philip Stone
    (Dad), Pauline Taylor (Psychiatrist), Margaret Tyzack (Conspirator),

Steven Berkoff (Constable), Lindsay Campbell (Inspector), Michael
Tarn (Pete), David Prowse (Julian), Jan Adair, Vivienne Chandler,
Prudence Drage (Handmaidens), John J. Carney (C.I.D. Man), Richard
Connaught (Billyboy), Carol Drinkwater (Nurse Feeley), Cheryl
Grunwald (Rape Girl), Gillian Hills (Sonietta), Virginia Wetherell
(Stage Actress), Katya Wyeth (Girl), Barrie Cookson, Gaye Brown,
Peter Burton, Lee Fox, Craig Hunter, Shirley Jaffe, Neil Wilson
RUNNING TIME: 137 minutes. Color

1975

BARRY LYNDON
SCRIPT: Stanley Kubrick, based on the novel by William Makepeace
    Thackeray
DIRECTOR: Stanley Kubrick
PHOTOGRAPHY: John Alcott
PRODUCTION DESIGNER: Ken Adam
EDITOR: Tony Lawson
MUSIC: Adapted and Conducted by Leonard Roseman, from works by
    Johann Sebastian Bach, George Friedrich Handel, Frederick the Great,
    Wolfgang Amadeus Mozart, Giovanni Paisiello, Franz Schubert and
    Antonio Vivaldi. Irish traditional music by The Chieftains
ART DIRECTOR: Roy Walker
COSTUMES: Ulla-Britt Soderlund
HISTORICAL ADVISER: John Mollo
PRODUCER: Stanley Kubrick
EXECUTIVE PRODUCER: Jan Harlan
ASSOCIATE PRODUCER: Bernard Williams
PRODUCTION COMPANY: Warner Bros./Hawk/Peregrine Films
DISTRIBUTOR: Warner Bros.
CAST: Ryan O'Neal (Barry Lyndon), Marisa Berenson (Lady Lyndon),
    Patrick Magee (Chevalier de Balibari), Hardy Kruger (Captain
    Potzdorf), Stephen Berkoff (Lord Ludd), Gay Hamilton (Nora Brady),
    Marie Kean (Mrs. Barry), Diana Koerner (Young German Woman),
    Murray Melvin (Reverend Samuel Runt), Frank Middlemass
    (Sir Charles Lyndon), André Morell (Lord Wendover), Arthur
    O'Sullivan (Highwayman), Godfrey Quigley (Captain Grogan),
    Leonard Rossiter (Captain Quinn), Philip Stone (Graham), Leon Vitali
    (Lord Bullingdon), Dominic Savage (Young Lord Bullingdon), David
    Morley (Little Bryan), Anthony Sharp (Lord Harlan), Pat Roach

(Toole), Norman Mitchell (Brock), Roger Booth (George III), Michael Hordern (Narrator)
RUNNING TIME: 187 minutes. Color

1980

THE SHINING
SCRIPT: Stanley Kubrick and Diane Johnson, based on the novel by Stephen King
DIRECTOR: Stanley Kubrick
PHOTOGRAPHY: John Alcott
STEADICAM OPERATOR: Garrett Brown
SOUND: Ivan Sharrock
EDITOR: Ray Lovejoy
PRODUCTION DESIGNER: Roy Walker
ART DIRECTOR: Les Tomkins
MAKEUP: Tom Smith
COSTUMES: Milena Canonero
MUSIC: Wendy Carlos and Rachel Elkind, György Ligeti, Béla Bartók, Krzysztof Penderecki
PRODUCER: Stanley Kubrick
EXECUTIVE PRODUCER: Jan Harlan
PRODUCTION COMPANY: Warner Bros./Hawk/Peregrine Films
DISTRIBUTOR: Warner Bros.
CAST: Jack Nicholson (Jack Torrance), Shelley Duvall (Wendy Torrance), Danny Lloyd (Danny), Scatman Crothers (Hallorann), Barry Nelson (Ullman), Philip Stone (Grady), Joe Turkel (Lloyd), Lia Beldam (Young Woman in Bathtub), Billie Gibson (Old Woman in Bathtub), Barry Dennen (Watson), David Baxt, Manning Redwood (Rangers), Lisa and Louise Burns (Grady Children), Kate Phelps (Receptionist), Allison Coleridge (Secretary), Burnell Tucker (Policeman), Jana Sheldon (Stewardess), Norman Gay (Injured Guest), Anne Jackson (Doctor), Tony Burton (Durkin)
RUNNING TIME: 142 minutes. Color

1987

FULL METAL JACKET
SCRIPT: Stanley Kubrick, Michael Herr, Gustav Hasford, based on the novel *The Short-Timers* by Gustav Hasford
DIRECTOR: Stanley Kubrick
PHOTOGRAPHY: Douglas Milsome

STEADICAM OPERATORS: John Ward, Jean-Marc Bringuier
EDITOR: Martin Hunter
COSTUMES: Keith Denny
PRODUCTION DESIGNER: Anton Furst
SET DRESSER: Stephen Simmonds
ORIGINAL MUSIC: Abigail Mead
ADDITIONAL MUSIC: Johnny Wright, Nancy Sinatra, The Dixie Cups, Sam the Sham and the Pharoahs, The Rolling Stones
SOUND: Nigel Galt, Edward Tise
ART DIRECTORS: Rod Stratford, Les Tomkins, Keith Pain
PRODUCER: Stanley Kubrick
EXECUTIVE PRODUCER: Jan Harlan
CO-PRODUCER: Philip Hobbs
ASSOCIATE PRODUCER: Michael Herr
PRODUCTION COMPANY: A Natant Film
DISTRIBUTOR: Warner Bros.
CAST: Matthew Modine (Private Joker), Adam Baldwin (Animal Mother), Vincent D'Onofrio (Private Pyle), Lee Ermey (Gunnery Sergeant Hartman), Dorian Harewood (Eightball), Arliss Howard (Private Cowboy), Kevin Major Howard (Rafter Man), Ed O'Ross (Lieutenant Touchdown), John Terry (Lieutenant Lockhart), Kieron Jecchinis (Crazy Earl), Kirk Taylor (Payback), Tim Colceri (Doorgunner), John Stafford (Doc Jay), Bruce Boa (Poge Colonel), Ian Tyler (Lieutenant Cleves), Gary Lanlon (Donlon), Sal Lopez (T.H.E. Rock), Papillon Soo Soo (Da Nang Hooker), Ngoc Le (Vietcong Sniper), Peter Edmound (Snowball), Tan Hung Francione (ARVN Pimp), Leanne Hong (Motorbike Hooker), Marcus D'Amico (Hand Job) Costas Dino Chimona (Chili), Gil Kopel (Stork), Keith Hodiak (Daddy Da), Peter Merrill (TV journalist), Herbert Norville (Daytona Dave), Nguyen Hue Phong (Camera Thief), Duc Hu Ta (Dead N.V.A.)
RUNNING TIME: 116 minutes. Color

1999

EYES WIDE SHUT
SCRIPT: Stanley Kubrick, Frederic Raphael, based on the novella *Traumnovelle* by Arthur Schnitzler
DIRECTOR: Stanley Kubrick
PHOTOGRAPHY: Larry Smith
STEADICAM OPERATORS: Elizabeth Ziegler, Peter Cavaciutti

EDITOR: Nigel Galt
PRODUCTION DESIGNERS: Les Tomkins, Roy Walker
ART DIRECTOR: John Fenner
COSTUME DESIGNER: Marit Allen
SOUND: Edward Tise
ORIGINAL MUSIC: Jocelyn Pook
ADDITIONAL MUSIC: György Liegeti, Dmitri Shastakovich, Chris Isaak
ORIGINAL PAINTINGS: Christiane Kubrick, Katharina Hobbs
PRODUCER: Stanley Kubrick
EXECUTIVE PRODUCER: Jan Harlan
COPRODUCER: Brian Cook
DISTRIBUTOR: Warner Bros
CAST: Tom Cruise (Dr. William Harford), Nicole Kidman (Alice
    Harford), Sydney Pollack (Victor Ziegler), Leslie Lowe (Illona), Peter
    Benson (Bandleader), Marie Richardson (Marion Nathanson), Rade
    Sherbedigia (Milich), Todd Field (Nick Nightingale), Vinessa Shaw
    (Domino), Alan Cumming (Hotel Desk Clerk), Sky Dumont (Sandor
    Szavost), Louise J. Taylor (Gayle), Stewart Thorndike (Nuala), Julienne
    Davis (Amanda "Mandy" Curran), Lisa Leone (Lisa, receptionist), Fay
    Masterson (Sally), Leelee Sobieski (Milich's Daughter), Thomas
    Gibson (Carl), Madison Eginton (Helena Harford), Jackie Sawris
    (Roz), Michael Doven (Ziegler's Secretary), Randall Paul (Harris),
    Kevin Connealy (Lou Nathanson), Mariana Hewett (Rosa), Leon
    Vitali (Red Cloak)
RUNNING TIME: 159 minutes. Color

Selected Bibliography

GENERAL STUDIES OF STANLEY KUBRICK

Baxter, John (1997). *Stanley Kubrick, A Biography*. New York: Carroll & Graf.

Chion, Michel (2001). *Kubrick's Cinema Odyssey*. London: British Film Institute.

Ciment, Michel (2001). *Kubrick: The Definitive Edition*. New York: Faber and Faber.

Coyle, Wallace (1980). *Stanley Kubrick: A Guide to References and Resources*. Boston: G. K. Hall.

DeVries, Daniel (1973). *The Films of Stanley Kubrick*. Grand Rapids, MI: William B. Eerdmans.

Falsetto, Mario (1994). *Stanley Kubrick: A Narrative and Stylistic Analysis*. Westport, CT: Praeger.

Falsetto, Mario, Ed. (1996). *Perspectives on Stanley Kubrick.* New York: G. K. Hall.

Howard, James (1999). *Stanley Kubrick Companion*. London: B. T. Batsford.

Hughes, David (2000). *The Complete Kubrick*. Forward by Peter Bogdanovich. London: Virgin Publishing.

Kagan, Norman (1996). *The Cinema of Stanley Kubrick*. New Expanded Edition. New York: Continuum.

Kerr, Michael (2000). *Kubrick*. New York: Grove Press.

Kolker, Robert (2000). *A Cinema of Loneliness: Penn, Stone, Kubrick, Scorsese, Spielberg, Altman*. New York: Oxford University Press, third edition.

LoBrutto, Vincent (1997). *Stanley Kubrick: A Biography*. New York: Penguin Books.

Mainar, Luis M. García (2000). *Narrative and Stylistic Patterns in the Films of Stanley Kubruck*. Rochester, NY: Camden House.

Nelson, Thomas Allen (2000). *Kubrick: Inside a Film Artist's Maze*. New and expanded edition. Bloomington: Indiana University Press.

Phillips, Gene D., Ed. (2001). *Stanley Kubrick: Interviews*. Jackson: University Press of Mississippi.

Pipolo, Tony (Spring 2002). "The Modernist and the Misanthrope: The Cinema of Stanley Kubrick." *Cineaste*, Vol. XXVII, no. 2, 41–5 and 49.

Walker, Alexander, Sybil Taylor, Ulrich Ruchti (1999). *Stanley Kubrick Director: A Visual Analysis*. Revised and expanded. New York: W. W. Norton.

THE SCREENPLAY

Kubrick, Stanley (1972). *Stanley Kubrick's Clockwork Orange, Based on the Novel by Anthony Burgess*. New York: Abelard-Schuman.

REVIEWS AND STUDIES OF *A Clockwork Orange*

Alpert, Hollis (December 25, 1971). "Milk-Plus and Ultra Violence." *Saturday Review*, no. 52, 40–41.

Barr, C. (Summer 1972). "*Straw Dogs, A Clockwork Orange*, and the Critics." *Screen* 13, no. 2, 17–31.

Boyers, Robert (Summer 1972). "Kubrick's *A Clockwork Orange*: Some Observations." *Film Heritage* 7, no. 4, 1–6.

Burgess, Anthony (February 17, 1972). "Clockwork Marmalade." *Listener* 87, no. 2238, 197–99.

Burgess, Anthony (June 8, 1972). "Juice from *A Clockwork Orange*." *Rolling Stone*, 52–53.

Burke, Tom (January 30, 1972). "Malcolm McDowell: The Liberals, They Hate 'Clockwork.'" *The New York Times*: Section 2, p. 13.

Canby, Vincent (January 9, 1972). "'Orange' – 'Disorienting But Human Comedy.'" *The New York Times*: Section 2, p. 7.

Collins, F. (1989). "Implied metaphor in the films of Stanley Kubrick." *New Orleans Review*, No. 16: 96–100.

Cocks, Jay (December 20, 1971). "Season's Greetings: Bang! Kubrick: Degrees of Madness." *Time*: 80.

Denby, David (March 1972). "Pop Nihilism at the Movies." *Atlantic*, 229, no. 3: 100–104.

Gow, Gordon (1974–75). "Novel into Film," in *Film Review*. edited by Maurice Speed. London: W. H. Allen, 1975: 33–42.

Gumenik, Arthur (Summer 1972). "*A Clockwork Orange*: Novel into Film." *Film Heritage*, 7, no. 4: 7–18 and 28.

Houston, Penelope (December 25, 1971)."Kubrick Country." *Saturday Review* 54, no. 52: 42–44.

Hughes, Robert (December 27, 1971)."The Décor of Tomorrow's Hell." *Time* 98, no. 26: 59.

Hutchings, William (March 1991). "'What's It Going to Be Then, Eh?'" The Stage Odyssey of Anthony Burgess's *A Clockwork Orange*." *Modern Drama*, no. 34: 34–48.

Issac, Neil D. (Spring 1973). "Unstuck in Time: *Clockwork Orange* and *Slaughterhouse Five*." *Literature/Film Quarterly* 1, no. 2: 122–131.

Kael, Pauline (January 1, 1972). "Stanley Strangelove." *The New Yorker* 48: 52–53.

Kauffmann, Stanley (January 1 and 8, 1972). "*A Clockwork Orange*." *The New Republic*: 22 and 32.

Kubrick, Stanley (February 27, 1972). "Now Kubrick Fights Back." *The New York Times*: Section 2, p. 1.

McCracken, Samuel (1973). "Novel Into Film, Novelist into Critic: *A Clockwork Orange*...Again." *Antioch Review* 32, no. 3: 427–36.

Mamber, Stephen (Winter 1973). "*A Clockwork Orange.*" *Cinema* [Los Angeles] 7, no. 3: 48–57.

Moskowitz, Ken (Winter 1977). "Clockwork Violence." *Sight and Sound* 46, no. 1: 22–23, 44.

Parmentier, Ernest (July 15, 1971). "A Clockwork Orange." *Filmfacts* 14, no. 24: 649–55.

Phillips, Gene (Winter 1972). "Kubrick." *Film Comment* 7, no. 4: 35–45.

Rice, Susan (March 1972). "Stanley Klockwork's 'Cubrick' Orange." *Media and Methods* 8, no. 7: 39–43.

Ricks, Christopher (April 6, 1972). "Horror Show." *New York Review of Books*: 28–31.

Riley, Clayton (January 9, 1972). "... Or 'A Dangerous, Criminally Irresponsible Horror Show?" *The New York Times*: Section 2, p. 1.

Samuel, Charles Thomas (Summer 1972). "The Context of *A Clockwork Orange.*" *American Scholar* 41, no. 3: 439–43.

Sarris, Andrew (December 30, 1971). "Films in Focus." *Village Voice* 16, no. 52: 49–50.

Schickel, Richard (February 4, 1972). "Future Shock and Family Affairs." *Life* 72, no. 4: 14.

Sklar, Robert (1988). "Stanley Kubrick and the American Film Industry." *Current Research in Film*, no. 4: 114–124.

Strick, Phillip (Winter 1972). "Kubrick's Horrorshow." *Sight and Sound* 41, no.1: 44–46.

Strick, Phillip, and Penelope Houston, (Spring, 1972). "Interview with Stanley Kubrick." *Sight and Sound* 41, no. 2: 62–66.

Wagner, Geoffrey (1975). *The Novel and the Cinema.* Madison, N.J.: Fairleigh Dickinson University Press: 307–13.

Walker, Beverly (1972). "From Novel to Film: Kubrick's *A Clockwork Orange.*" *Women and Film* 2: 4.

Zimmerman, Paul D. (January 3, 1972). "Kubrick's Brilliant Vision." *Newsweek* 79, no. 1: 29.

Index